Unleash Greatness in Your Child

Powerful, Character–Building, Positive Parenting Activities

An "I Care" Positive Parenting Workbook

No part of this "I Care" *Unleash the Greatness in Your Child* Workbook may be reproduced in whole or in part, or stored in a retrieval system, or transmitted in any form or by any means electronic, mechanical, photocopied, recorded, or otherwise without express written permission of the publisher, "I Care" Products & Services.

Schools and school systems **do not** have permission to copy any part of this book for use as instructional material. Each Workbook is intended for individual use.

All of the logos, artwork, designs, and activities in this Workbook are exclusively owned by "I Care" Products & Services and are protected under copyright law.

Written by Elbert D. Solomon, Thelma S. Solomon, and Martha Ray Dean
Book design and illustrations by Phillip L. Harper, Jr.

ISBN: 1-891187-06-6
4th Grade; First Edition
Copyright© June, 2006 by "I Care" Products & Services
E-mail: parents7@icarenow.com
www.icarenow.com/parents.html
All rights reserved. Printed in the U.S.A.

Table of Contents

Introduction . . . . *ii*
How To Use This Book . . . . *iii*
"I Care" Positive Parenting
  Workbooks . . . . *v*
A Proven Educational Method . . . . *vi*
"I Care" Positive Parenting Pledge . . *vii*
"I Care" Positive Child's Pledge . . . . *ix*

January — Persistence — 1

Parenting Activities *1*
Enrichment Activities *5*
Reinforcement Activity *10*
Reflection Activity *11*

February — Monitor Thinking — 13

Parenting Activities *13*
Enrichment Activities *17*
Reinforcement Activity *22*
Reflection Activity *23*

March — The Value of Appreciation — 25

Parenting Activities *25*
Enrichment Activities *29*
Reinforcement Activity *34*
Reflection Activity *35*

April — The Value of Forgiveness — 37

Parenting Activities *37*
Enrichment Activities *41*
Reinforcement Activity *46*
Reflection Activity *47*

May — Endurance — 49

Parenting Activities *49*
Enrichment Activities *53*
Reinforcement Activity *58*
Reflection Activity *59*

June — Be Generous — 61

Parenting Activities *61*
Enrichment Activities *65*
Reinforcement Activity *70*
Reflection Activity *71*

July — Be Thorough — 73

Parenting Activities *73*
Enrichment Activities *77*
Reinforcement Activity *82*
Reflection Activity *83*

August — The Value of Thriftiness — 85

Parenting Activities *85*
Enrichment Activities *89*
Reinforcement Activity *94*
Reflection Activity *95*

September — Be Creative Through Reading — 97

Parenting Activities *97*
Enrichment Activities *101*
Reinforcement Activity *108*
Reflection Activity *109*

October — Be Joyful — 111

Parenting Activities *111*
Enrichment Activities *115*
Reinforcement Activity *122*
Reflection Activity *123*

November — Have Honor — 125

Parenting Activities *125*
Enrichment Activities *129*
Reinforcement Activity *134*
Reflection Activity *135*

December — Be Reliable — 137

Parenting Activities *137*
Enrichment Activities *141*
Reinforcement Activity *146*
Reflection Activity *147*

Recommended Books *149*
Workbook Series *150*
50 Ways Parents Can Say "I Care" . . *151*
"I Care" Parental Involvement Book . *152*

Introduction

The "Unleash the Greatness in Your Child" Workbook
The "Unleash the Greatness in Your Child" Workbook will not only increase the impact that you can have on the social, emotional, and academic growth of your children, but it can help them to reach their fullest potential. Highly successful individuals share a number of traits in common. Among them are the thinking skills, attitudes, and behavior patterns that represent "character." This book provides tools for parents like you who want to begin unleashing the potential in their children through the development of their character.

Positive Parenting
Positive parenting strengthens parent/child relationships by engaging children with the most important teachers they will ever have—their parents. Furthermore, it increases academic achievement and expectations for the future; instills self–esteem and confidence; and reduces behavior problems and school absenteeism.

Character Development
Character development doesn't just happen, it is primarily learned from role models and significant adults and should be started at an early age. A list of the twelve "Pillars of Character" upon which the "I Care" approach is based is found on pages iv and v, along with the behaviors that define them at each grade level of the "I Care" Positive Parenting Workbooks.

"I Care"
Beginning over ten years ago, "I Care" is committed to communicating with parents the importance of their involvement with their children and helping them improve their parenting skills. Today, "I Care" is used by over a million parents.

"I Care" Positive Parenting & Mentoring Curricula
"I Care" Positive Parenting & Mentoring Curricula are used in over 35,000 classrooms for Toddler and Pre–K through High School. Activities similar to the ones in this Workbook are implemented by parents throughout the school year. Administrators, teachers, and parents have all raved about the results.

Feedback
Feedback is one of the key components to the "I Care" approach. Defining parental involvement as the number of positive interactions you have with your child makes it easy. The *Reflection Activity* at the end of each month will help you keep track of your involvement. The other indicator will be the changes you see in your child. They will be stunning.

How To Use This Book

Practice, Practice, Practice
Practice is necessary for a behavior or attitude to become a habit. That's why we provide so many activities for each character trait. In fact, learning theory tells us that it generally takes 21 days of practice before a new habit is acquired. But don't stop with ours! Be creative in developing your own activities as well.

Discuss, Discuss, Discuss
Discuss—not tell, tell, tell—is the rule. If a child can talk about an idea using his own words, ask questions about it, and consider it from different points of view, he will both learn it and understand it more completely.

Parenting Activities
Carefully read through the month's activities. Designate a visible location to place the positive message and post the activities (refrigerator, message board, etc.). The activities can be done while walking or riding in the car, at the breakfast table, at bedtime, on weekends, and in other situations where you and your child are together. Take advantage of the "teachable moments" and read to and with your child daily.

Monthly Character Traits
There are twelve important character traits, one for each month of the year, spiraling from a Pillar of Character. They instill self–esteem, positive attitudes, and self–confidence. Focus on one character trait per month and complete the associated parenting, enrichment, reinforcement, positive message (monthly character trait), and reflection activities.

Parenting Pledge
The *Parenting Pledge* is an affirmation from the parent to the child that the character traits will be practiced and reinforced. Display it in a visible location. (See page vii.)

Child's Pledge
The *Child's Pledge* is an affirmation from the child to the parents. Have your child repeat it often until it is committed to memory. Display it in your child's room. (See page ix.)

Enrichment Activities
The *Enrichment Activities* will get your child excited and motivated about learning. The activities are designed to enhance your child's skills in reading, writing, constructing, designing, recognizing, visualizing, making patterns, and communicating.

Positive Messages
The monthly *Positive Message* should be displayed in a visible location to help your

child maintain focus on one character trait while you, as a parent, provide reinforcement actions.

Reinforcement Activities
These *Reinforcement Activities* will give parent and child multiple opportunities to manipulate and model the behaviors associated with each character trait during the month.

Reading Activities
The recommended books and reading activities support the child's literacy development and reinforce the monthly character traits. These books may be available at your local library or they can be purchased in a set of 12 at www.icarenow.com/parents.html. Other books that reinforce the month's concept may be used if the recommended books are unavailable.

Reflection Activity
The monthly *Reflection Activity* is designed for parents to summarize their positive actions, recognize their accomplishments, and encourage self–initiation of more positive parent/child interactions.

Successful Parenting Practices
The timeless successful parenting practices at the end of each month's activities were used as a guide to develop the "I Care" Positive Parenting Workbook. They serve as models for effective parent/child relationships.

12 Universal Pillars of Character

Goal Setting—*Learning How to Plan*

Self–Aware—*Understanding What You Think and Why*

Value Achievement—*Taking Pride in Accomplishments*

Value Others—*Being Able to See the Good in Everyone*

Self–Control—*Keeping Action and Emotion in Check*

Caring—*Respecting Others' Feelings and Giving of One's Self*

Responsible—*Following Through on Commitments*

Citizenship—*Showing Loyalty to the Rights of Others*

Life–Long Learner—*Enhancing Learning Skills*

Self–Confidence—*Trusting in Your Own Abilities*

Respect—*Showing Honor or Esteem*

Trustworthiness—*Being Honest*

"I Care" Positive Parenting Workbooks

- Built on twelve universally recognized pillars of good character with spiraling grade–level character traits to build one behavior on another
- Includes the primary behaviors that define each character trait for the repetition that enables transfer of learning
- Includes parenting/mentoring, enrichment, reinforcement, visual learning, and reflection activities
- Additional grade–level workbooks are available for the grades listed below

Month	Pillars of Character	Pre-K	Kindergarten	1st Grade	2nd Grade	3rd Grade	4th Grade	5th Grade	6th Grade
January	Goal-Setting	Dream	Dream	Imagine	Hard Work	Persevere	Persist	Set Goals	Plan
February	Self-Aware	Recognize Feelings	Recognize Feelings	Sensitive	Humility	Consistency	Monitor Thinking	Integrity	Set Personal Standards
March	Value Achievement	Recognize Achievement	Recognize Achievement	Accomplishments	Accept Recognition	Dedication	Appreciation	Productive Thinking	Push Limits of Abilities
April	Value Others	Unique Qualities	Unique Qualities	Make Friends	Value Differences	Hospitable	Forgiveness	Loyalty	Tolerance
May	Self-Control	Self-Control	Self-Control	Self-Discipline	Cautious	Punctual	Endurance	Control Impulses	Respond to Feedback
June	Caring	Caring	Caring	Respect	Compassion	Gentle	Generous	Sympathetic	Dependability
July	Responsible	Responsible	Responsible	Follow Procedures	Dependable	Prudence	Thorough	Accuracy	Willing to Accept Blame
August	Citizenship	Positive Attitude Toward School	Positive Attitude Toward School	School Pride	Oversee Environment	Understand Consequences	Thriftiness	Cooperation	Stands for Right
September	Life-Long Learner	Read	Read	Discover	Listen	Alertness	Creative	Find Facts	Express Feelings
October	Self-Confidence	Self-Confidence	Self-Confidence	Self-Reliance	Optimism	Courage	Joyful	Problem Solving	Right Choices
November	Respect	Courteous	Courteous	Polite	Fairness	Patience	Honor	Open-Minded	Positive Attitude
December	Trustworthy	Honest	Honest	Sincere	Loyalty	Truthful	Reliable	Self-Knowledge	Virtuous

Copyright© 2006 "I Care" Products & Services (4th Grade)

Do Not Photocopy

v

A Proven Educational Method

"I Care" follows best strategies of the teaching and learning process described below and has been professionally developed using relevant research.

Advanced Organizers
The *Message to Parents* is provided for introducing the month's character trait.

Three Essential Learning Conditions
These have been identified by cognitive psychologists and embedded into the workbook: reception, availability, and activation.
1. Reception—Advanced organizers focus the child's attention on specific activities.
2. Availability—Parents can take advantage of the "teachable moments" and insert parenting activities into the home schedule at any time.
3. Activation—When parents role model the character traits and ask questions such as those provided in the preplanned activities, they are activating the child's cognitive assimilation of the trait.

Repetition, Repetition, Repetition
Long–term memory is enhanced by the number of times a child mentally manipulates a trait. "I Care" provides varied repetitions of each character trait over an extended period of time. Learning theory tells us that it generally takes 21 days of practice before a new habit is acquired.

Use of Questioning Strategies
Most of the "I Care" Activities are written in the form of open–ended questions.

Connected to Real Life
Children are able to respond to activity questions (passive activity) utilizing their own experiences, and when activities involve doing something (active activity), children carry out the activity within a familiar environment that is part of their daily lives.

Substantive Conversation
Research shows that a child must talk about an idea or trait using his or her own words, ask questions about it, and look at it from multiple points of view for it to be assimilated to the point that the trait transfers into automatic behavior response. The "I Care" Workbook has built–in opportunities for all these kinds of conversations.

"I Care" Positive Parenting Pledge

I Pledge To Teach My Child:

The Importance of Persistence

How to Monitor Thinking

The Value of Showing Appreciation

The Value of Forgiveness

The Importance of Endurance

How to Be Generous

How to Be Thorough

The Importance of Thriftiness

How to Be Creative

How to Be Joyful

How to Have Honor

The Importance of Being Reliable

Tear out this page and display the Parenting Pledge on the other side in a visible location.

Do Not Photocopy. Copyright© 2006 "I Care" Products & Services (4th Grade)

"I Care" Positive Child's Pledge

I Pledge To:

Do My Best to Achieve in School

Read Daily for Information or Enjoyment

Have a Positive Attitude Toward School

Listen to My Parent's Advice

Use Good Manners

Practice Common Courtesies

Limit My Television Watching

Be Responsible for My Actions

Stick With a Task Until It Is Finished

Tear out this page and display the Child's Pledge on the other side in a visible location.

Do Not Photocopy. Copyright© 2006 "I Care" Products & Services (4th Grade)

Persistence

January

Parenting Activities

Message to Parents

Children understand persistence. How many children do you know who keep begging until they get what they want or interrupting until you stop what you are doing so that you can talk to them? The key is to channel persistence toward positive goals through positive behavior.

1. COMMUNICATION
Persistence Pays Off

Watch the movie *The Rookie* with your child. Use the example of the father who followed his dream to become a baseball player to discuss persistence. On page 5, you will find some of the behaviors that go along with positive persistence.

2. ROLE PLAYING
Model It

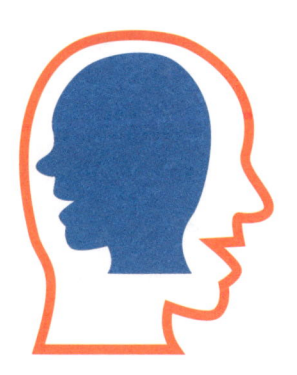

Demonstrate to your child how breaking down a large task into small steps makes the task seem less challenging. This makes it easier to persist to completion. Examples might be working on a school report or completing a home improvement project. You can share the saying "How do you eat an elephant?" (One bite at a time.)

January — **Persistence**

Parenting Activities

3. TABLE TALK
Talk About It

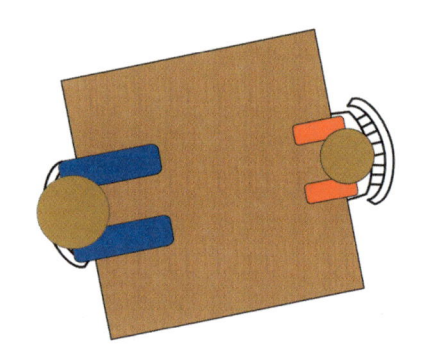

Discuss the following with your child:
- "Most of the important things in the world have been accomplished by people who have kept on trying when there seemed to be no hope at all."
  —Dale Carnegie, Author of *How to Win Friends and Influence People*
- "Let me tell you the secret that has led me to my goal: my strength lies solely in my tenacity."
  —Louis Pasteur, discoverer of antiseptic techniques and rabies vaccine
- "Whoever said anybody has a right to give up?"
  —Marian Write Edelman, founder of the *Children's Defense Fund*

4. WRITING
You Can Do It

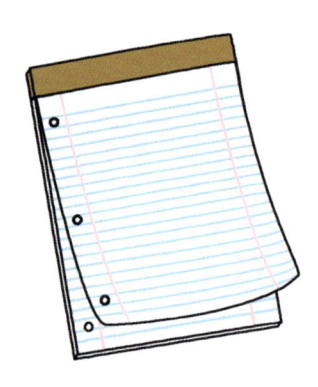

No one is too old for Dr. Seuss. Read *Horton Hatches an Egg* with your child. You'll find it at the library. Talk about Horton's persistence, then challenge your child to write a story of a character that shows persistence, that has a "can do" and "I won't quit" attitude. It might be a make believe character, an animal, or a child. Share the story with the family.

Persistence

Parenting Activities

5. PHYSICAL
Time and Effort

Have your child identify a skill in which he needs to develop greater accuracy. Examples could be piano sight–reading, volleyball serving, adding fractions, or learning Spanish pronunciation. Have him write down the improvement he wants to make within four weeks. He should practice at least three times a week and evaluate how much his accuracy improved at the end of the month. If he reaches his goal, celebrate! If not, was it because the goal was too big, or because he didn't practice enough? The point is that developing accuracy takes time and effort.

6. READING
Courage and Determination

Sadako and the Thousand Paper Cranes, by Eleanor Coerr, is the true story of a young Japanese girl whose courage and determination are an inspiration. Ask your child to imagine the kind of persistence Sadako had. Are there challenges he faces that require the same kind of persistence? Talk about them.

January — Persistence

Parenting Activities

7. COMMUNITY
Letter of Appreciation

Help your child find an example of someone who has persisted in your community for the benefit of others. Is there someone who has campaigned to build a community center or park? How about volunteers for a local charity? Do you have a friend who is always there to lend a helping hand? Have your child send a letter thanking that person for his persistence.

Positive Parenting Practices

If it's difficult for your child to maintain his concentration and persist to the completion of a task, let him take a break, play some music, run around outside for 15 minutes, or get a drink of water. Then, he can return to finish the task.

Persistence

Enrichment Activity

Activity 1: Communication–Persistence Pays Off

Use the fact sheet below for the *Communication Activity* on page 1.

If you are persistent, you will . . .

- Always finish what you start, even if you have to work a little harder or a little longer to get the job done.
- Make sacrifices in order to reach your goal, like turning off the TV to study because you want to get good grades, practicing twice as long as usual to memorize a new piano piece, giving up snacks to save money for something special.
- Try again and again when something doesn't work right the first time.
- Keep working at something that is difficult until you complete it.

Examples of Persistent People:
- *Beethoven, a composer, was deaf.*
- *Stevie Wonder, a musician, is blind.*
- *Albert Einstein, a great scientist, had a learning disability.*
- *James Earl Jones, the voice of Darth Vader and actor, had to overcome stuttering.*
- *Helen Keller, an author, was deaf and blind.*
- *Franklin D. Roosevelt, President of the United States, was paralyzed by polio.*

Copyright© 2006 "I Care" Products & Services   (4th Grade)   Do Not Photocopy.

Persistence

Enrichment Activity

Activity 2: Project–Practice Persistence

It takes persistence to reach a goal. Practice as a family. Have each person select a goal they can complete in a week. Write everyone's goal on a large piece of paper with a large circle underneath each. Demonstrate how each person will fill in a pie–shaped piece of the circle each time they work on their goal, using a different colored marker for each slice of the pie. When the goal is reached, the circle will be filled in. If all the circles are filled in at the end of the week, have a popcorn celebration. If they aren't filled in, talk about why and how to be more persistent on the next goal. Do this on a regular basis.

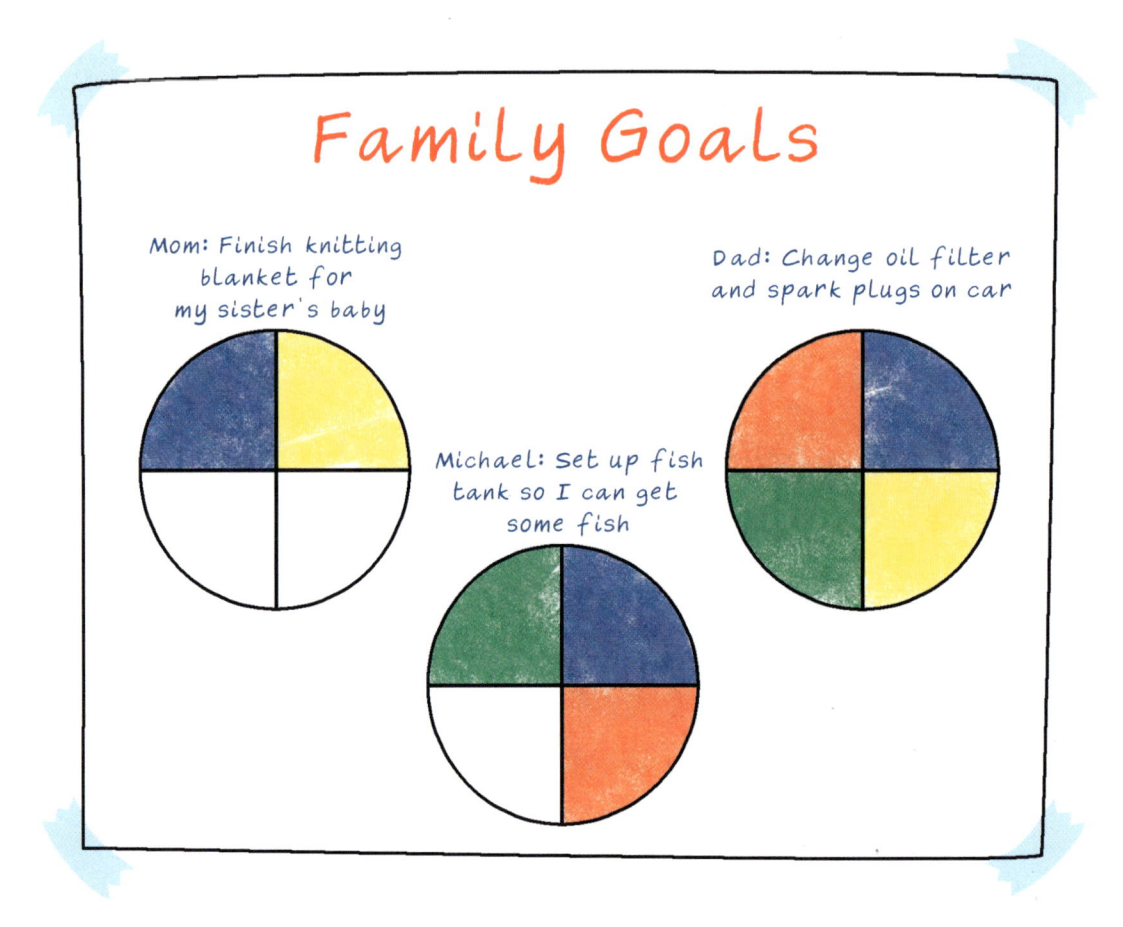

Family Goals

Mom: Finish knitting blanket for my sister's baby

Dad: Change oil filter and spark plugs on car

Michael: Set up fish tank so I can get some fish

Persistence

Enrichment Activity

Activity 3: Art—Origami

Have you ever tried origami? Try it with your child. Follow the instructions for making a paper crane at the end of this month's book, *Sadako and the Thousand Paper Cranes*. How did it turn out? Persist until your creation looks like the crane on page 79 of the book (book included in Recommended Book Pack; see page 149). You can use the square on the next page as a template for your crane.

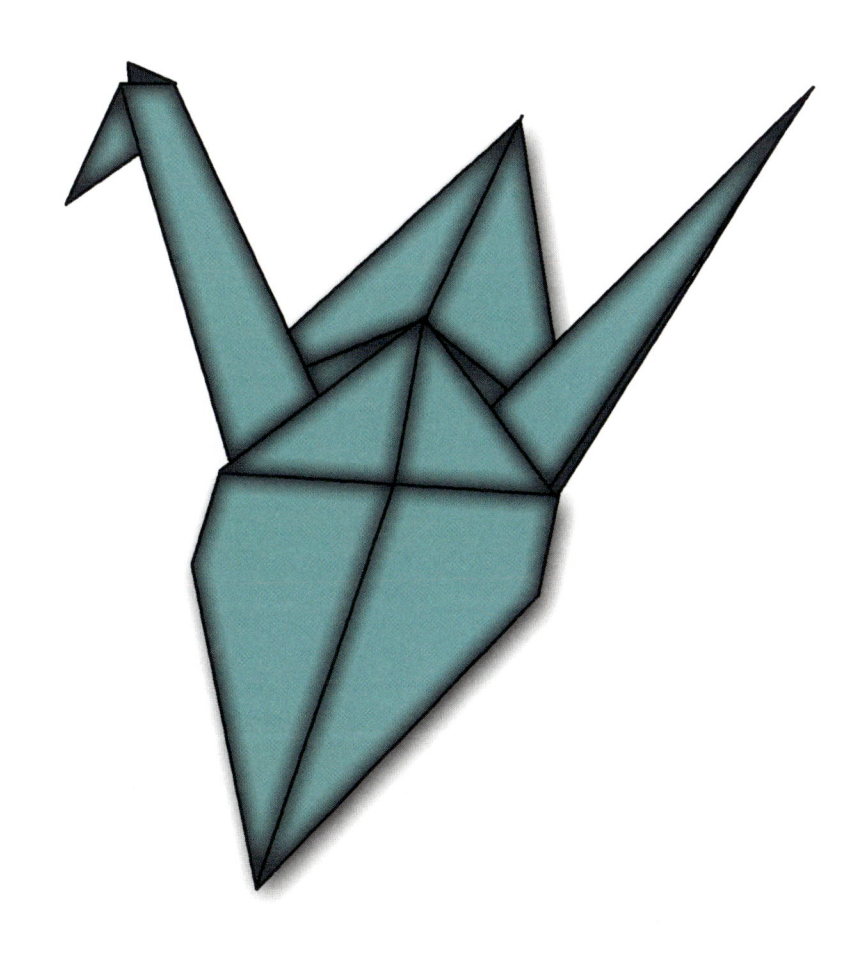

January

Persistence

8

Do Not Photocopy.   Copyright© 2006 "I Care" Products & Services   (4th Grade)

Persistence

January

Positive Message

Activity 4: Visual Learning

Discuss with your child the positive message below. Post the message in a visible location for your child to see it often during the month. At the end of the month, complete *Activity 5* on the other side of this sheet.

With persistence, you can accomplish much.

Copyright© 2006 "I Care" Products & Services   (4th Grade)

Do Not Photocopy.

January

Persistence

Reinforcement Activity

Activity 5: Things I Am Persistent At . . .

Record the things your child is persistent at and post in a visible location.

1. _____

2. _____

3. _____

4. _____

5. _____

Persistence

January

Reflection Activity

Activity 6: Reflection Log

Summarize your child's positive interactions during the month and reward yourself for a job well done.

Child's Name _____ **Date** _____

Name of Parent(s) _____

Record the number for each of the following questions in the box on the right.

A. How many of the workbook activities did you do with your child? ☐

B. How many positive recognitions did your child receive from teacher(s)? ☐

C. How many positive recognitions did your child receive from family members, friends, etc.? ☐

D. How many positive recognitions did your child receive from you, the parent(s)? ☐

Copyright© 2006 "I Care" Products & Services   (4th Grade)   Do Not Photocopy.

January

Persistence

D. Record five self-initiated positive activities you did with your child that were not in this month's workbook activities.

1. _____
   _____

2. _____
   _____

3. _____
   _____

4. _____
   _____

5. _____
   _____

Monitor Thinking

February

Parenting Activities

Message to Parents

Today's children grow up in a world of visual orientation, multitasking, constant noise, and immediate gratification. Helping children become aware of what they think and why will increase their reflective thinking.

1. COMMUNICATION
Think About Thinking

Talk with your child about what it's like to monitor one's thinking. It's knowing what you are thinking and why you are thinking it. This is important because you may discover what you're thinking is inaccurate, or that your opinion is based on wrong information. You can't make corrections if you don't know what you're thinking in the first place. Thinking about thinking also helps children learn better.

2. ROLE PLAYING
Model It

Do a lot of thinking out loud as you are reading, writing, or after listening to the news. You might say "Is this accurate? How could I say this another way? Am I making any assumptions? Why do I believe that is true? Is that based on fact or feeling?"

Monitor Thinking

Parenting Activities

3. TABLE TALK
Talk About It

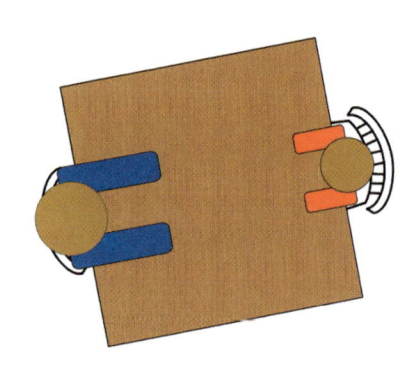

Discuss the following with your child:
- What are some of the things that worry you? What can you do about it?
- What do you say to yourself when you're having a hard time doing something? If it's not a "can do" statement, change what you are saying.
- It's okay to talk to yourself when you are learning something new. That may help you to remember it.
- Here are some things to ask yourself while you are studying: What information is important to remember? Should I read slower if the information is hard to understand? What do I need to do if I do not understand?

4. WRITING
Here's What I Think

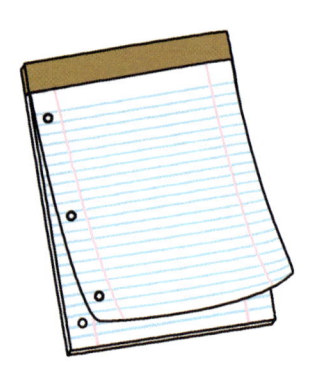

On page 17, you'll find some sentences, each with blanks in it. Have your child fill in the blanks, then talk about her answers. This will help her become more aware of what she thinks and why.

Monitor Thinking

Parenting Activities

5. PHYSICAL
Time It

When your child is doing something that is hard for her, try this. Set a timer to go off every five or ten minutes. When it does, ask her what she's thinking. If it is something like "This is really hard, I don't think I can do it. Why do I have to do this anyway?," encourage her to change her thinking. Ask her to instead say "This may be hard, but I know I can do it. Slow and steady wins the race. This will be worth it in the end." Research says that attitude is 85% of achievement.

6. READING
Coping and Understanding

A Taste of Blackberries, by Doris Buchanan Smith, tells the story of a young boy who must learn to cope with the death of his best friend. As you read the book with your child, point out the kinds of questions the boy asked himself as he struggled to understand what had happened. Asking yourself questions is one way to monitor thinking.

February

Parenting Activities

Monitor Thinking

7. COMMUNITY
Hot or Cold

The old game of "20 Questions" can exercise your child's thinking. She has to retain facts in her short-term memory and analyze them in order to come up with the correct answer. As you are traveling in the car, ask her to guess different people, places, or things in the community. If you need to brush up on the rules of the game, see page 18.

Positive Parenting Practices

Ask questions that require your child to explain and justify her thinking.

16
Do Not Photocopy.

Copyright© 2006 "I Care" Products & Services (4th Grade)

Monitor Thinking

Enrichment Activity

Activity 1: Writing—Here's What I Think

Use the worksheet below for the *Writing Activity* on page 14.

The most important thing I do is _____ *because* _____.

I really don't like to _____ *because* _____.

I am proud when I _____ *because* _____.

I know a lot about _____.

I will always remember when I _____ *because* _____.

I get worried about my homework when _____ *because* _____.

I know I'm on the right track when _____ *because* _____.

I know I need to change the way I'm doing something when _____ *because* _____.

Monitor Thinking

Activity 2: Community—"20 Questions"

Use the instructions below for the *Community Activity* on page 16.

1. Think of a person, place, or thing in the community.

2. Have your child ask questions about the person, place, or thing that can be answered with a "Yes" or "No."

3. Answer questions by saying either "Yes" or "No" without saying anything else.

4. After each answer, she can try to guess the person, place, or thing.

5. The questions she asks will indicate the complexity of her thinking. Does she start with questions that will narrow down the possible answers quickly, such as size or whether the object moves or contains something, and save the detail questions for last? If she asks questions that don't help narrow the options quickly, point that out.

6. To get her started, you can tell her if it is an animal, vegetable, or mineral. After that, she is on her own.

Monitor Thinking

Enrichment Activity

February

Activity 3: Project–Job Aid

Help your child practice some strategies that will increase her thinking and understanding, using the list below. Tear out this page and post it where your child does her homework. Review them from time to time.

Ways to Increase Thinking and Understanding

Am I on Track?
Double check homework directions. Make sure they are followed.

What Will It Look Like?
If I do the assignment correctly, what will it look like? Did my teacher show me some examples?

Study Buddy
Talk with someone about what I am studying: "This is what I understand . . . . Tell me what you understand."

Know Already–Want to Learn–Learned (K–W–L)
When starting to study a new subject, list two or three of the facts I already know about it. Then, write something I'd like to learn. That will help me to pay attention as I study. When I'm finished, did I learn what I wanted to learn?

Mark It
While I am reading something new, it can help to put symbols into the text to indicate (1) I know that, (2) I'm confused, (3) I disagree, (I didn't know that). If most of the symbols say "I'm confused," You probably need to talk with someone about what you read. If the symbols say "I disagree," the next thing you need to do is ask yourself why you disagree. Maybe you need to change your opinion.

What Do You Think?
While studying new information, write down some of the new facts you learned and what you thought about them. You can use the "T–Chart" on the next page. Writing your opinion actually helps you remember the facts.

Portfolio
Collect samples of your work. You will be able to see how you are getting better at expressing your ideas clearly or writing good paragraphs. They can also help you decide on things you need to improve, like spelling or grammar.

February

Monitor Thinking

New Fact	What I Think

Monitor Thinking

Positive Message

February

Activity 4: Visual Learning

Discuss with your child the positive message below. Post the message in a visible location for your child to see it often during the month. At the end of the month, complete *Activity 5* on the other side of this sheet.

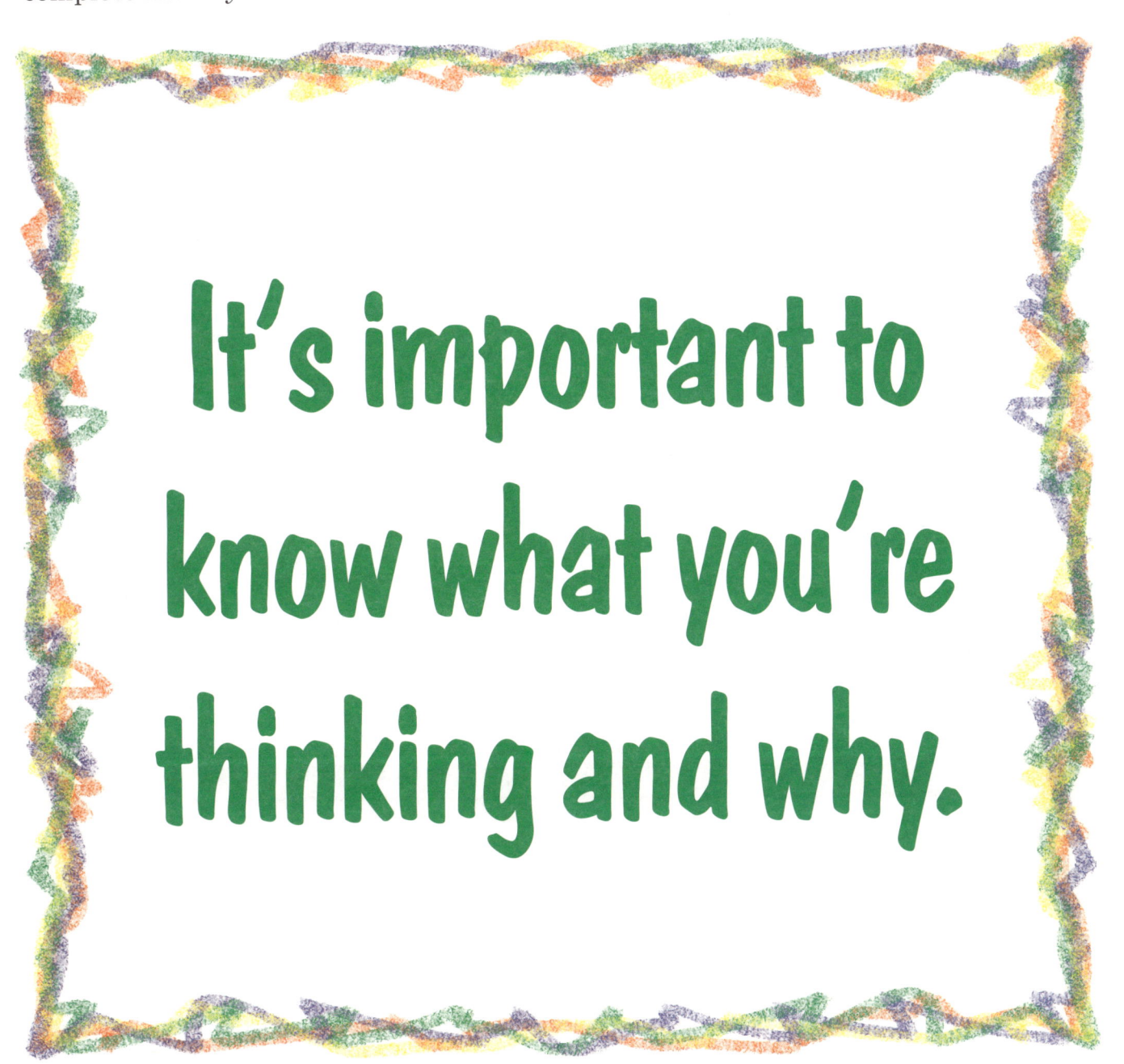

It's important to know what you're thinking and why.

February

Monitor Thinking

Reinforcement Activity

Activity 5: Times I Monitor Thinking . . .

Record some times/situations when you monitor your child's thinking.

1. _____

2. _____

3. _____

4. _____

5. _____

Do Not Photocopy.   Copyright© 2006 "I Care" Products & Services   (4th Grade)

Monitor Thinking

Reflection Activity

February

Activity 6: Reflection Log

Summarize your child's positive interactions during the month and reward yourself for a job well done.

Child's Name _____ **Date** _____

Name of Parent(s) _____

Record the number for each of the following questions in the box on the right.

A. How many of the workbook activities did you do with your child? ☐

B. How many positive recognitions did your child receive from teacher(s)? ☐

C. How many positive recognitions did your child receive from family members, friends, etc.? ☐

D. How many positive recognitions did your child receive from you, the parent(s)? ☐

February

Monitor Thinking

D. Record five self–initiated positive activities you did with your child that were not in this month's workbook activities.

1. _____
   _____

2. _____
   _____

3. _____
   _____

4. _____
   _____

5. _____
   _____

The Value of Appreciation

Parenting Activities

Message to Parents

We're living in what has been called "The Age of Entitlement." People feel that they are owed whatever they want. Children believe that it's their parents' job to provide it. Instead of catering to their children, parents need to help them recognize the quality, value, and significance of people and things.

1. COMMUNICATION
In Our Family

Gather any recognitions that have been received by your child or family members (ribbons, awards, certificates, trophies, etc.). Discuss what they mean and how they were earned.

2. ROLE PLAYING
Model It

Recognize and compliment family members often for the positive things they do. Write notes to each other and put them in surprise places to be discovered later, such as in book bags, books, pockets, purses, shoes, etc.

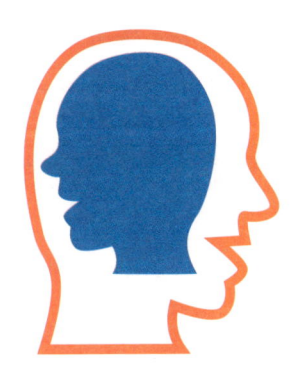

Parenting Activities

3. TABLE TALK

Talk About It

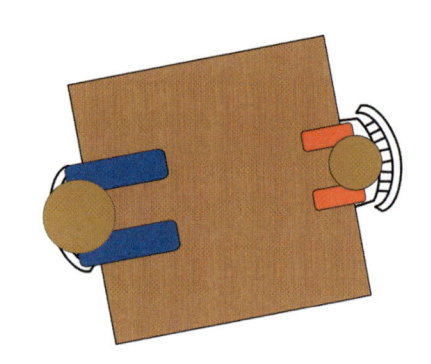

Discuss the following with your child:
- What are some of the ways you can show appreciation to (family members/friends)?
- How do good manners show appreciation?
- How can you show people you appreciate their opinions without necessarily agreeing with them?
- *Talk about the following quotes: "There is more hunger for love and appreciation in the world than there is for bread."—Mother Theresa*
  "Imitation is the sincerest form of flattery."—Author unknown

4. WRITING

Family Biography

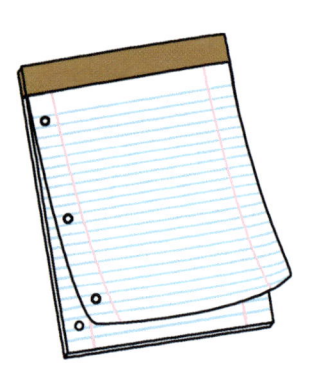

The more we know about our families, the more we can appreciate some of the things they went through and value the sacrifices they made for their children and grandchildren. Help your child become a family historian, recording stories of the past and sharing them with everyone. On page 29, you'll find some tips for writing a family biography.

The Value of Appreciation

Parenting Activities

5. PHYSICAL
What Was It Like?

Rent the PBS special *Frontier House* and watch it with your family. It will surely give you an appreciation for how easy our lives are now. Talk with your family about whether you would be brave enough to volunteer for a project like the families in the show, living like pioneers did in 1880. Then, try a pioneer meal. Milk and "hoecakes" is all some people might have to eat. They'd take flour or corn meal with them into the field, mix it with water, and cook it on the flat side of a shovel or hoe over a fire. Make your "hoecakes" with one cup of whole wheat flour or corn meal and a pinch of salt mixed with enough water to make dough. Pat it into a thin cake and fry it in a skillet. That and a cup of milk or coffee is all you get!

6. READING
Show Appreciation

Sarah Ida learns one lesson in appreciation after another—some of them that force her to stretch beyond what she thought she could do. As her friend Al tells her, "Maybe you don't want to do it, but you'll feel better in after years." After reading *Shoeshine Girl*, by Clyde Robert Bulla with your child, talk about how showing appreciation, even when it's hard or inconvenient, may be something he will value even more when he's older.

March — The Value of Appreciation

Parenting Activities

7. COMMUNITY
Show of Appreciation

Imagine with your child what it was like to live through "The Great Depression" and through World War II. Most of our senior citizens did. Arrange with a local nursing home for your child, along with some of his friends, to have a "Show of Appreciation" honoring them for their contributions to their families and communities. Give each a certificate of appreciation designed in the *Art Activity* for this month.

Positive Parenting Practices

- Show appreciation to your child by listening to him, asking his opinion, and involving him in making some family decisions.

- Establish family traditions for showing appreciation for one another and for what you have. Share what you're grateful for and make this a daily routine.

Do Not Photocopy. Copyright© 2006 "I Care" Products & Services (4th Grade)

The Value of Appreciation

Enrichment Activity

Activity 1: Writing—Being a Family Historian

Use the information below for the *Writing Activity* on page 26.

How to Get the Information
- Pick a few people who know the details and ask if you can interview them.
- Have a tape recorder or video and blank tapes. Test the volume.
- Before each interview, tell who is being interviewed, your name, the purpose of the interview, and the date.
- Ask questions and give the person plenty of time to answer.
- Thank the person when you are finished.

Questions You Might Ask
- Describe what things were like when you were growing up.
- What did you like to do as a child?
- What games or toys did you like best?
- What was school like for you?
- What did you like best about school? Least?
- Who was your best friend?
- What did you do together?
- Is there a family story you would like us to always remember?

Now What?
- You can make copies of the tapes or videos for everyone in your family.
- Make a booklet of some of the most interesting facts or stories. You can include photocopies of pictures if some are available. Make copies of the booklet and share it with family and friends.

Enrichment Activity

The Value of Appreciation

Activity 2: Art–Certificate of Appreciation

Design certificates of appreciation that can be awarded to senior citizens for their long life of giving. You'll find lots of examples by doing an on-line search for "certificates of appreciation." You may want to make several designs. Make copies and fill them in for each person who will be at the Show of Appreciation in the *Community Activity* on page 28.

Certificate of Appreciation

Presented to:
Aunt Mary
For her love
and generosity

Yeah!

The Value of Appreciation

Enrichment Activity

March

Activity 3: Project—My Family

Help your child become the family historian if there isn't one already. Plan a trip to a location of significance to your family. Share any heirlooms you have. Tell the stories behind them. Talk about ethnic heritage and customs. Pass on family values, beliefs, hopes, and dreams. Help your child organize what information is available into a family scrapbook, containing the family biography from the *Writing Activity* on page 26, pictures, awards, copies of old records, a family tree, etc. Keep adding to it.

The Value of Appreciation

Activity 4: Project-Show Appreciation

Appreciation is the recognition of value, quality, and magnitude of people and things. Teach your child to always look for opportunities to recognize others for jobs done well. The simplest and most impactful way to let someone know you appreciate them is to say "Thank you." Below is a list of additional ways.

- Send a card of appreciation
- Give or send a gift
- Include someone in a team activity
- Vocally praise someone in a public gathering
- Support a project someone else is doing
- Submit someone's name for a special award
- Purchase lunch, dinner, or snacks for someone
- Share books, music, games, etc.

The Value of Appreciation

Positive Message

March

Activity 4: Visual Learning

Discuss with your child the positive message below. Post the message in a visible location for your child to see it often during the month. At the end of the month, complete *Activity 5* on the other side of this sheet.

Look for opportunities to compliment others for a job well done.

Copyright© 2006 "I Care" Products & Services   (4th Grade)

Do Not Photocopy.

Reinforcement Activity

The Value of Appreciation

Activity 5: Times I Showed Appreciation

Record times your child showed appreciation to others and post in a visible location.

1. _____

2. _____

3. _____

4. _____

5. _____

The Value of Appreciation

Reflection Activity

March

Activity 6: Reflection Log

Summarize your child's positive interactions during the month and reward yourself for a job well done.

Child's Name _____ **Date** _____

Name of Parent(s) _____

Record the number for each of the following questions in the box on the right.

A. How many of the workbook activities did you do with your child? ☐

B. How many positive recognitions did your child receive from teacher(s)? ☐

C. How many positive recognitions did your child receive from family members, friends, etc.? ☐

D. How many positive recognitions did your child receive from you, the parent(s)? ☐

Copyright© 2006 "I Care" Products & Services   (4th Grade)   Do Not Photocopy.

March

The Value of Appreciation

D. Record five self–initiated positive activities you did with your child that were not in this month's workbook activities.

1. _____

2. _____

3. _____

4. _____

5. _____

The Value of Forgiveness

Parenting Activities

April

Message to Parents

Forgiveness is more than the act of saying "I'm sorry." When you apologize, it requires the humility and desire to make up for any harm that was done. When you accept an apology, it's with the understanding that everyone makes mistakes.

1. COMMUNICATION
Forgive for Your Own Sake

Forgiveness isn't just polite, it's healthy. Talk with your child about how holding a grudge means that the other person is still in control of your emotions and that's not healthy. Forgiving someone can reduce stress and lead to a greater feeling of well–being and peace. Try an experiment to make the point. Close your eyes and imagine a person who hurt or angered you. After about 20 seconds, did your heart beat faster? Now, imagine taking those feelings and throwing them as far away as you can. Are you starting to relax?

2. ROLE PLAYING
Model It

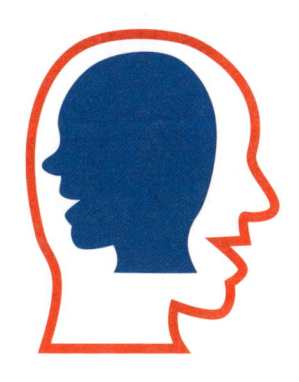

Model forgiveness with family members and friends. Be forgiving and forgive others. Ask your child to forgive you when it is appropriate. Don't hesitate to tell your child you're sorry about something. Also, show your child that it's good to forgive yourself.

Copyright© 2006 "I Care" Products & Services   (4th Grade)

April

The Value of Forgiveness

Parenting Activities

3. TABLE TALK
Talk About It

Discuss the following with your child:
- Why is it important to forgive people?
- *Talk with your child about the following quotes:*
  "Forgiveness is not an occasional act; it is a permanent attitude."—Martin Luther King, Jr.
  "Resentment is like drinking poison and then hoping it will kill your enemies."—Nelson Mandela

4. WRITING
What Would You Say?

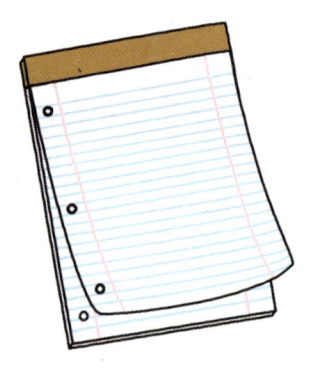

Have your child write a conversation between two friends, one who is apologizing to the other for hurting her feelings. Have her include what each might say.

The Value of Forgiveness

Parenting Activities

5. PHYSICAL
Practice

Teach your child to apologize in a sincere manner. When offering an apology, your child should be specific about what she's done wrong. For example: "I'm sorry I hurt your feelings when I called you stupid. Will you forgive me?" Also teach your child to properly accept an apology from someone else by saying something like the following: "I accept your apology." Practice so that it becomes automatic.

6. READING
Overcoming Bitterness

Caleb's Story, by Patricia MacLachlan, is a sequel to *Sarah, Plain and Tall*. In it, Caleb helps his grandfather overcome bitterness from the past, forgive, and begin to look forward to the future. After reading it with your child, share about someone you might have known who was able to forgive and move on. What positive impact resulted from showing forgiveness?

April — The Value of Forgiveness

Parenting Activities

7. COMMUNITY

Apologize or Not?

For all of history, people have been taking land from each other. It happened where you live. Ask the local librarian for help in finding out the early history of your community. Who were the first recorded inhabitants? Who came and settled on their land? Recently, the U.S. government passed an "Apology Bill" acknowledging past abuses to all Native Peoples. Talk to your child about whether someone should apologize to the ancestors of the original inhabitants of your community. Where does forgiveness come in?

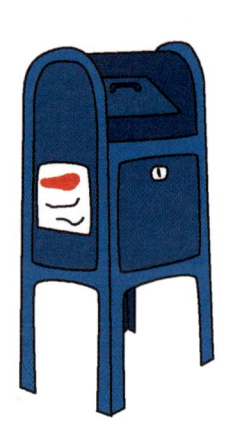

Positive Parenting Practices

Natural and logical consequences and making amends by parents and children are expected, but this needs to be accomplished in an atmosphere of forgiveness.

The Value of Forgiveness

Enrichment Activity

Activity 1: Project—Can You Imagine?

Anne Frank is an amazing example of forgiveness. Read about her and some of the things she said below. Talk with your child about what it must have been like for Anne and what might have made it possible for her to be so forgiving of the people who were persecuting her.

Anne Frank was a German-Jewish teenager who, with her family and some friends, spent two years hiding from the Nazis in two rooms above her father's office in Amsterdam, Netherlands. After being betrayed by a Dutch collaborator, they were all sent to concentration camps. In March of 1945, nine months after she was arrested, and just weeks before the camps were liberated, Anne Frank died of typhus. She was fifteen years old.

Her diary was saved during the war by one of the family's helpers and later published by her father, the only family member to survive the Holocaust. Today, her diary has been translated into 67 languages and is one of the most widely read books in the world. Below are a few excerpts.

"It's a wonder I haven't abandoned all my ideals, they seem too absurd and impractical. Yet I cling to them because I still believe, in spite of everything, that people are truly good at heart."

"And yet, when I look up at the sky, I somehow feel that everything will change for the better, that this cruelty too shall end, that peace and tranquility will return once more."

"How lovely that everyone great and small can make their contribution toward justice . . . . And you can always, always give something even if it is only kindness."

April

Enrichment Activity

The Value of Forgiveness

Activity 2: Art—What Forgiveness Looks Like

What do people look like when they are showing forgiveness? Talk with your child about humility and how it is related to forgiveness. Then, ask your child to draw in the box below her impression of what someone would look like if he was forgiving someone else.

Do Not Photocopy.   Copyright© 2006 "I Care" Products & Services   (4th Grade)

The Value of Forgiveness

Enrichment Activity

April

Activity 3: Project—How to Mend a Broken Heart

When your child is involved in a heartfelt situation, you can help her mend her broken heart. Ask her to share the situation and describe what she considers to be the most desirable positive outcomes. Document her responses on the heart below. Cut out the heart pieces and tape them together. Reverse the heart and hang it in a visible location.

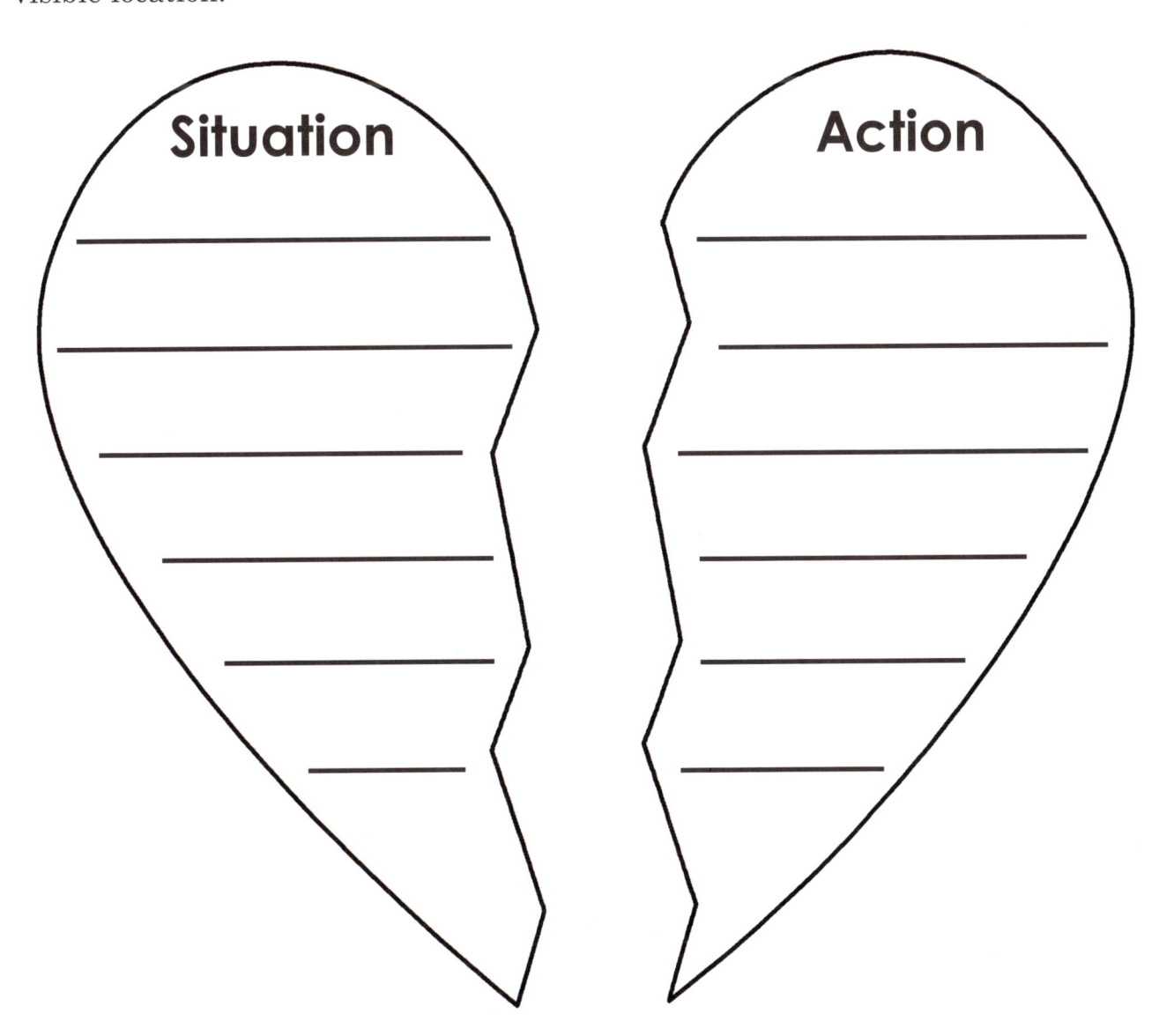

Situation

Action

April

The Value of Forgiveness

Cut out the heart halves on the other side of this page for the Project Activity.

FOR GIVEN

44
Do Not Photocopy. Copyright© 2006 "I Care" Products & Services (4th Grade)

The Value of Forgiveness

Positive Message

April

Activity 5: Visual Learning

Discuss with your child the positive message below. Post the message in a visible location for your child to see it often during the month. At the end of the month, complete *Activity 6* on the other side of this sheet.

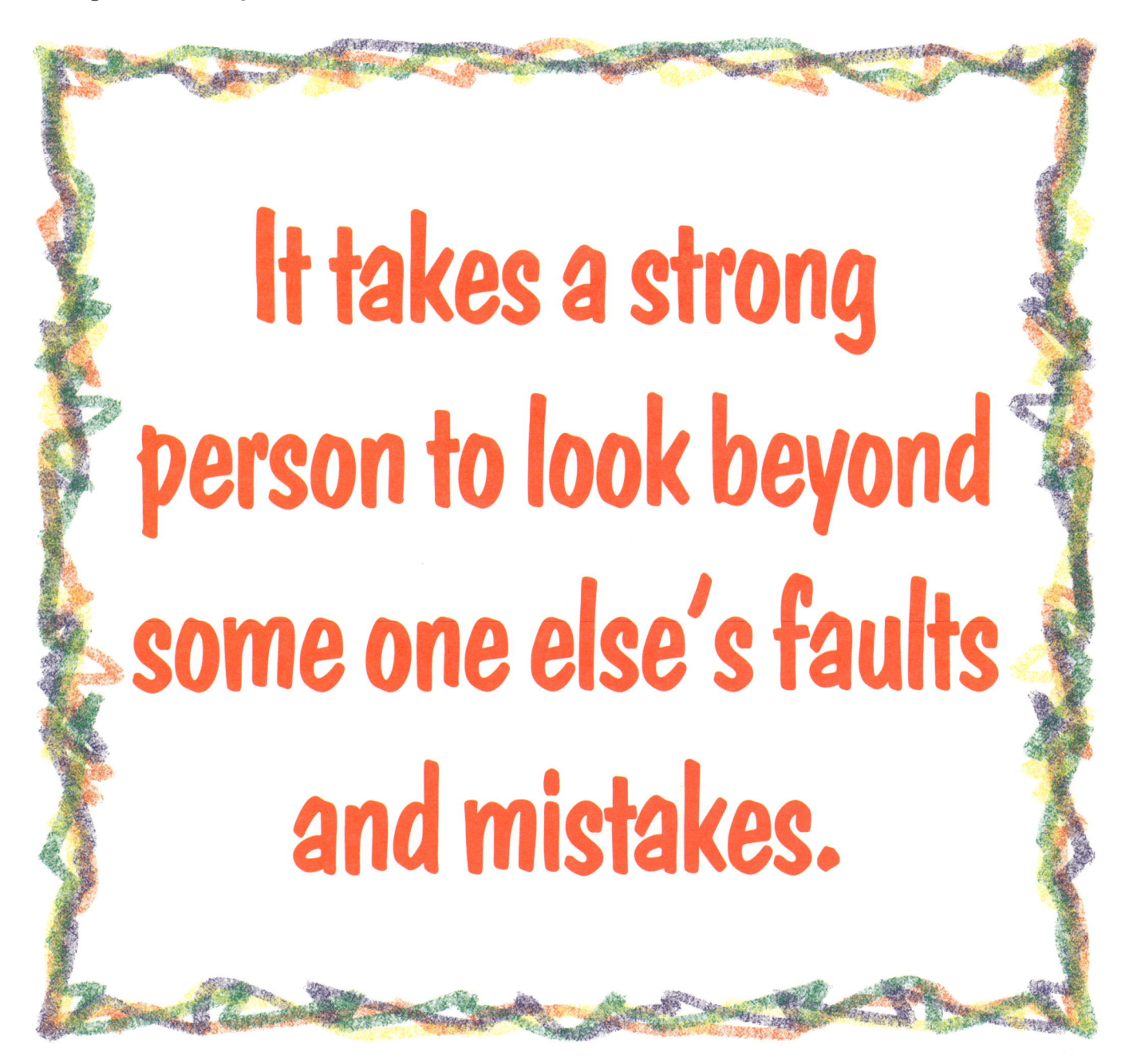

It takes a strong person to look beyond some one else's faults and mistakes.

April

Reinforcement Activity

The Value of Forgiveness

Activity 6: When I Forgive . . .

Record times when your child demonstrated forgiveness and post in a visible location.

1. _____

2. _____

3. _____

4. _____

5. _____

The Value of Forgiveness

Reflection Activity

April

Activity 7: Reflection Log

Summarize your child's positive interactions during the month and reward yourself for a job well done.

Child's Name _____ **Date** _____

Name of Parent(s) _____

Record the number for each of the following questions in the box on the right.

A. How many of the workbook activities did you do with your child? ☐

B. How many positive recognitions did your child receive from teacher(s)? ☐

C. How many positive recognitions did your child receive from family members, friends, etc.? ☐

D. How many positive recognitions did your child receive from you, the parent(s)? ☐

The Value of Forgiveness

D. Record five self-initiated positive activities you did with your child that were not in this month's workbook activities.

1. _____

_____

2. _____

_____

3. _____

_____

4. _____

_____

5. _____

_____

Endurance

Parenting Activities

Message to Parents

We usually think of endurance as the power to withstand physical hardship. But there are other kinds of endurance. Patiently waiting out a difficult situation or remaining calm under stress are a few examples.

1. COMMUNICATION
Make a Record

With your child, ask some senior citizens to share stories of endurance. You may even want to video or tape record what they say as oral history. Times are changing and it's wise to remember what those who live before us have endured.

2. ROLE PLAYING
Model It

Parents are often a model of endurance for their children. This is especially true of immigrant parents or those seeking to increase financial security for their families. These parents endure long hours and multiple jobs so life will be better for their children. How are you a model of endurance?

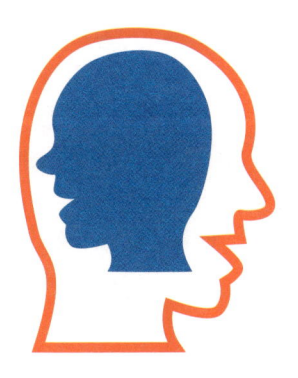

Parenting Activities

Endurance

3. TABLE TALK

Talk About It

Discuss the following with your child:
- Endurance is one of the most difficult disciplines, but it is to the one who endures that the final victory comes.
- Endurance is patience concentrated.
- A lie has speed, but the truth has endurance.

4. WRITING

The Rest of the Story

Sea of Ice: The Wreck of the Endurance, by Monica Kulling, tells the story of an expedition to cross the continent of Antarctica and the unbelievable hardships the explorers endured. Check this book out of the library and read it with your child. There's also an HBO movie called *The Endurance*. At the very least, read the fact sheet on page 53 and search for "Ernest Shackleton" on–line. Have your child write a story about being a stowaway on the *Endurance*. Encourage him to share it with his class at school.

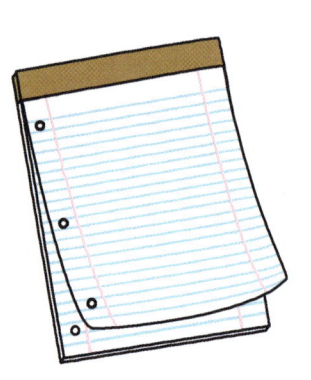

Endurance

Parenting Activities

5. PHYSICAL
Build Your Endurance

Lance Armstrong and his seven victories in the *Tour de France* bicycle race is one of the best examples of physical endurance we have today. The key to his success is training and attitude. On page 54, you'll find some of his tips. Go over these with your child. Help him build up his endurance. Go walking with him throughout the month. Increase the pace and/or length of your walk. Maybe this will become part of your weekly routine.

6. READING
Shape Up!

Judge and Jury are two brothers who love to have fun—too much fun according to their mother, who threatens to send Judge to another school if he doesn't "shape up." Enjoy reading *Egg Drop Blues*, by Jacqueline Turner Banks, with your child, especially the challenges the boys endure. Talk about how growing up involves risking new things and learning to endure.

Endurance

Parenting Activities

7. COMMUNITY
Join the Race

May is the time of year that a lot of community organizations sponsor races and relays. *The Cancer Society* has the *Relay for Life*, and there are relays, races, and marathons to raise money for almost any disease. Check with your local Chamber of Commerce to find a race you can participate in with your family. Running and jogging are not required. The goal is to finish. How good is your endurance?

Positive Parenting Practices

When teaching endurance to children, the emphasis should be on the process, not how long you can last.

Endurance

Activity 1: Writing–The Endurance

Use the information below for the *Writing Activity* on page 50.

Ernest Shackleton and the *Endurance*

Ernest Shackleton was an Irishman born in 1874 who went to sea at age 16, and at age 24, he was a certified commander. By 1901, he was part of an expedition to explore the Antarctic. He's credited with placing a famous ad in the *Times of London* to recruit men for the expedition. It read: *"Men wanted for hazardous journey. Small wages. Bitter cold. Long months of complete darkness. Constant danger. Safe return doubtful. Honour and recognition in case of success."* Illness prevented Shackleton from completing that expedition, but he later headed several of his own.

The best known was the *Imperial Trans–Antarctic Expedition* that set out in 1914 to cross the continent of Antarctica, passing through the South Pole. Because of poor planning, the inexperience of the men, and the assumption that they could succeed on will power alone, they had to abandon their goal before they even got started. Their ship, the *Endurance*, became stuck and was crushed by the ice. They then went by sled and boat. The story of their journey is legendary for the hardships they endured and the ingenuity they used in rebuilding their small boat so it could survive an ocean voyage to get help. Six men left in that 21 foot boat. The rest of the crew remained on Elephant Island for 22 months awaiting rescue. Miraculously, everyone survived.

Endurance

Activity 2: Physical–Lance Armstrong Says . . .

Use the information below for the *Physical Activity* on page 51.

- *Planning is important—Think ahead about what you want to do. Finishing strong is the goal, not starting strong.*

- *Think strong. Get strong—Keep a positive attitude.*

- *Mix up your intensity—Don't keep working really hard all the time or you'll wear yourself out.*

- *Take your fitness seriously—Make sure you are in good shape. Exercise.*

- *Know your strengths and weaknesses—If you are really good at something, figure out how to do that more. Practice to strengthen your weaknesses.*

Endurance

Enrichment Activity

Activity 3: Art—Endurance Award

Movie stars receive *Oscars*. Heroes get medals. Have your child create a three dimensional award that can be given to the seniors she interviews in the *Communication Activity* on page 49. Encourage him to be creative. He can use play dough or craft clay, make a banner, or paint a wooden plaque. He could include the name of the person receiving the award, as well as why it's being given.

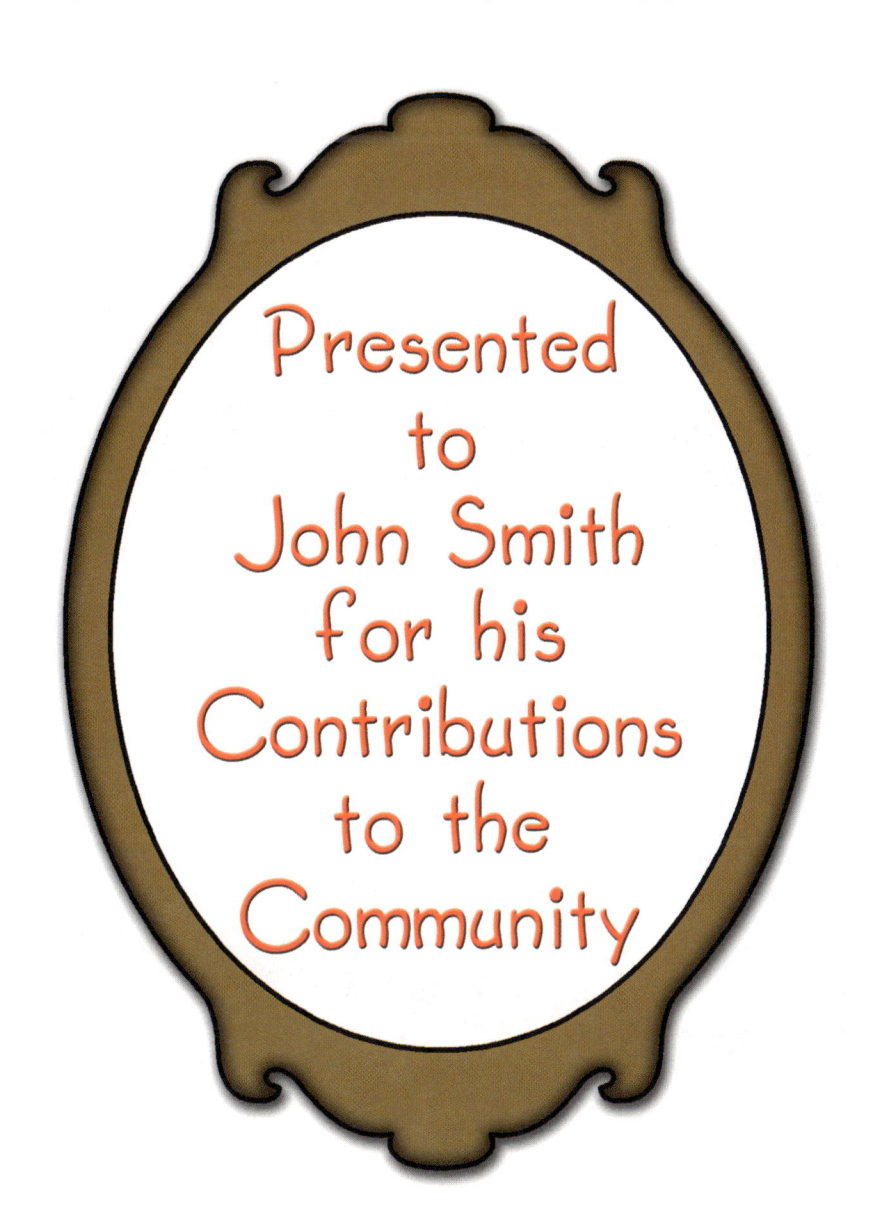

Presented to
John Smith
for his
Contributions
to the
Community

Endurance

Activity 4: Project-I Have Endurance

There is a television show called *Endurance* on the Discover Channel. It features teams of teenagers competing against each other in one challenge of endurance after another, until only one team is left. Anyone between ages 13 and 18 can apply to be on the show by submitting a five-minute long video telling about himself or herself and why he or she is applying to be on the show. After watching an episode, have your child imagine he is applying to be on the show. He can make a video or present his case to the family. Creativity is encouraged, music is not allowed. Endurance should be stressed. Did he make his case well enough to be selected?

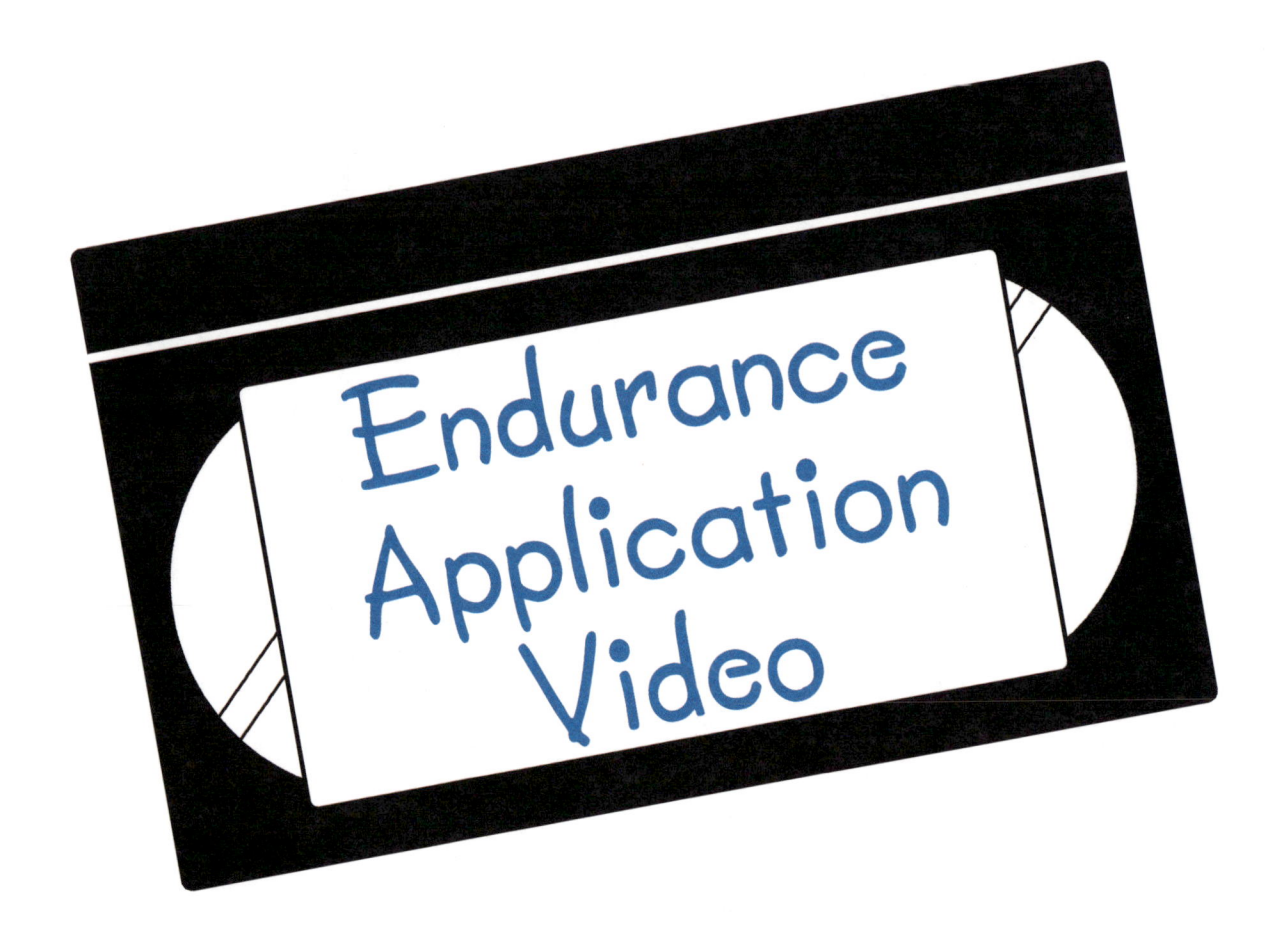

Endurance

Positive Message

Activity 5: Visual Learning

Discuss with your child the positive message below. Post the message in a visible location for your child to see it often during the month. At the end of the month, complete *Activity 6* on the other side of this sheet.

Think strongly. You can do it!

Endurance

Reinforcement Activity

Activity 6: It Takes Endurance to . . .

Record examples of times when your child demonstrated endurance and post in a visible location.

1. _____

2. _____

3. _____

4. _____

5. _____

Endurance

May

Reflection Activity

Activity 7: Reflection Log

Summarize your child's positive interactions during the month and reward yourself for a job well done.

Child's Name _____ **Date** _____

Name of Parent(s) _____

Record the number for each of the following questions in the box on the right.

A. How many of the workbook activities did you do with your child?

B. How many positive recognitions did your child receive from teacher(s)?

C. How many positive recognitions did your child receive from family members, friends, etc.?

D. How many positive recognitions did your child receive from you, the parent(s)?

Copyright© 2006 "I Care" Products & Services (4th Grade)

Do Not Photocopy.

May

Endurance

D. Record five self–initiated positive activities you did with your child that were not in this month's workbook activities.

1. _____

   _____

2. _____

   _____

3. _____

   _____

4. _____

   _____

5. _____

   _____

Be Generous

June

Parenting Activities

Message to Parents

Help your child become a cheerful giver; someone who enjoys giving in order to help others, not because she expects to get something in return. Generous people tend to have more meaningful relationships and make a greater contribution to society.

1. COMMUNICATION
Ways to Show Generosity

Generosity isn't just giving gifts. There are many other behaviors that represent a generous nature. Examples are listed on page 65. Go over these with your child and add some of your own. Talk about the generous things she does besides giving gifts.

2. ROLE PLAYING
Model It

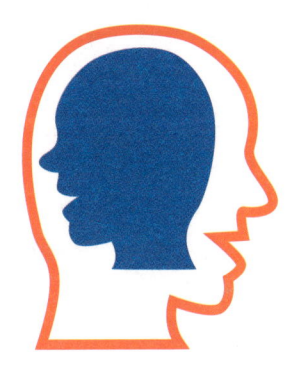

Be sure your child knows when you give your time, money, and advice to others. Be sure to talk about why you do such things so your child will understand that you are concerned about the needs and feelings of others. You can even let your child help select some of the family giving projects.

Be Generous

Parenting Activities

3. TABLE TALK
Talk About It

Discuss the following with your child:
- What if you wanted to invite the new student in your class to eat with you at lunch, but the other kids didn't. What could you do?
- *Hold each other accountable to help someone each week or a few people a month and share these during family time.*

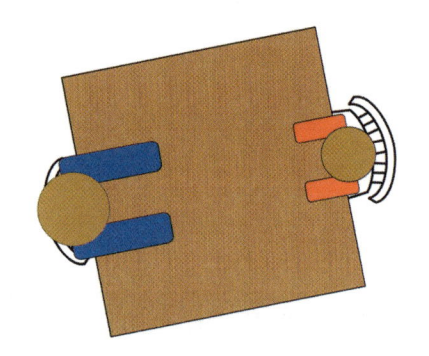

4. WRITING
Generosity

There are some wonderful stories about generosity, such as *The Quiltmaker's Gift*, by Jeff Brumbeau, and *The Giving Tree*, by Shel Silverstein. Read one of these or another story you know with your child and talk about how generous the characters are or aren't. Have her write a story about the most generous thing she's ever done and share it with the family.

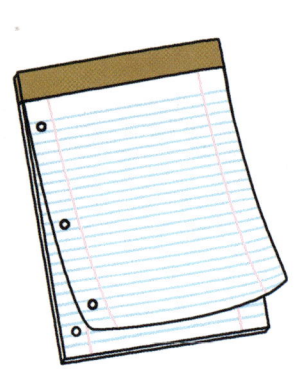

Be Generous

Parenting Activities

5. PHYSICAL
Giving Time and Attention

During the month, arrange for your child to either spend time with elderly relatives or talk to them on the phone regularly. Suggest some things she might want to share with them.

6. READING
Generosity of Spirit

The Hundred Penny Box, by Sharon Bell Mathis, is a story about Michael, who learns a lesson in generosity of spirit as he protects and defends his great–great Aunt Dew. After reading the book with your child, ask her to visualize some of the scenes from the book, especially the last one. What was it like for Michael as he was stretched out by Aunt Dew and she was calling him John, the name of her long–dead husband? What was Aunt Dew imagining?

June — Be Generous

Parenting Activities

7. COMMUNITY
Give Away

Have your child ask family members and friends to look through their closets and find items of clothing to donate to local charitable organizations. Encourage each person to give at least one item he would like to keep for himself.

Positive Parenting Practices

While you're teaching generosity, don't be surprised if your child suddenly makes you feel guilty for not giving more. Just remember, it's also an important lesson for your child to learn the limits of what you *can* give.

Generous

Enrichment Activity

Activity 1: Communication—Ways to Show Generosity

Use the information below for the *Communication Activity* on page 61.

- Cooperate with others and be polite to everyone all of the time.

- When you see someone who is being left out of a group, ask him to join you.

- Try to understand why someone hurt your feelings instead of striking back.

- Keep a good attitude when your parents ask you to do something. Do it right away.

- Play fair and be a good sport if you lose.

- _____

- _____

- _____

- _____

- _____

- _____

June

Be Generous

Parenting Activities

Activity 2: Project-Giving Brigade

Help your child establish a "Giving Brigade," a collection of friends, family, and neighbors who regularly identify people in need and find a way to help them. By involving other people, you can share the work and help more people. The "Brigade" could meet once every few months, pick some people to help, and decide who is going to do what. Examples of help might be taking an elderly neighbor to the doctor, taking groceries to a friend who is sick, collecting food for the local food pantry, etc.

Be Generous

Enrichment Activity

JUNE

Activity 3: Project–Set the Example

Let your child see you giving the U.S. Postal Service and/or community organizations canned foods that will be used to feed the poor and hungry. Help your child cut out the labels below and ask her to write some notes of encouragement and tape them on the cans.

Example:

| These beans are very good! Enjoy them! |

| |

| |

| |

| |

June

Be Generous

Cut out the labels on the other side of this page for the Project Activity.

68
Do Not Photocopy. Copyright© 2006 "I Care" Products & Services (4th Grade)

Be Generous

Positive Message

Activity 4: Visual Learning

Discuss with your child the positive message below. Post the message in a visible location for your child to see it often during the month. At the end of the month, complete *Activity 5* on the other side of this sheet.

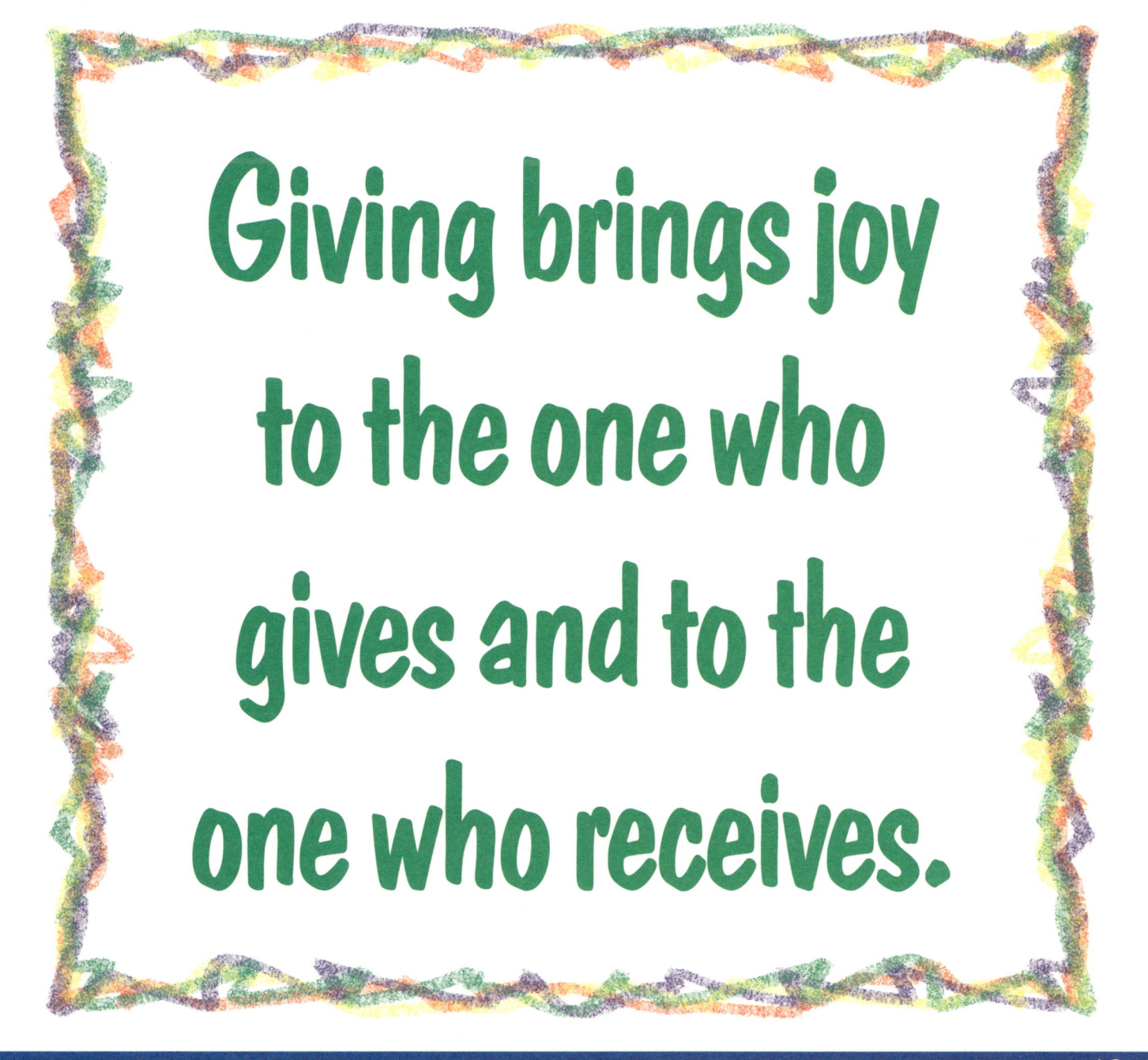

> # Giving brings joy to the one who gives and to the one who receives.

Be Generous

Reinforcement Activity

Activity 5: Being Generous to Others . . .

Record examples of times your child was generous to others and post in a visible location.

1. _____

2. _____

3. _____

4. _____

5. _____

Be Generous

Reflection Activity

June

Activity 6: Reflection Log

Summarize your child's positive interactions during the month and reward yourself for a job well done.

Child's Name _____ **Date** _____

Name of Parent(s) _____

Record the number for each of the following questions in the box on the right.

A. How many of the workbook activities did you do with your child? ☐

B. How many positive recognitions did your child receive from teacher(s)? ☐

C. How many positive recognitions did your child receive from family members, friends, etc.? ☐

D. How many positive recognitions did your child receive from you, the parent(s)? ☐

Copyright© 2006 "I Care" Products & Services (4th Grade)   Do Not Photocopy.

June

Be Generous

D. Record five self–initiated positive activities you did with your child that were not in this month's workbook activities.

1. _____
   _____

2. _____
   _____

3. _____
   _____

4. _____
   _____

5. _____
   _____

Be Thorough

July

Parenting Activities

Message to Parents

In today's society, being thorough is more important than ever. There are just simply more details to manage. Learning to be thorough at a young age will enable your child to avoid pitfalls in the future.

1. COMMUNICATION
Consequences

One way to teach a concept is to illustrate it with negative examples. Talk to your child about the consequences of *not* being thorough. Examples: your new house has termites because you didn't do a thorough house inspection; the new recipe didn't turn out right because you left out one of the ingredients; you ran out of food at the party because you didn't anticipate extra guests; etc. Talk about some of the things your child needs to do thoroughly.

2. ROLE PLAYING
Model It

Be aware of the things you do that can model thoroughness for your child. They can be as simple as wiping the table and vacuuming the floor to more complex jobs of planning a vacation, planting a garden, or buying the right appliance. Use self–talk (talking to yourself aloud) to point out why it's important to be thorough.

Be Thorough

Parenting Activities

3. TABLE TALK
Talk About It

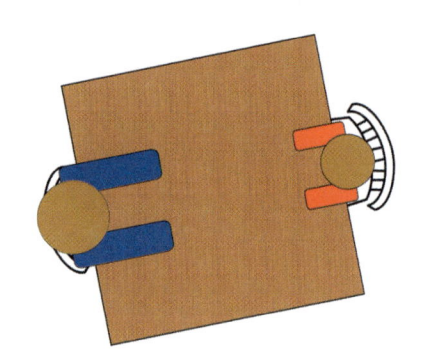

Discuss the following with your child:
- What does the following quote mean? *"Thorough preparation makes it's own luck."*—Joe Poyer
- What are some of the things you do thoroughly?
- How do you know when someone has not done a thorough job of planning, studying, or cleaning up?

4. WRITING
Thorough Planning

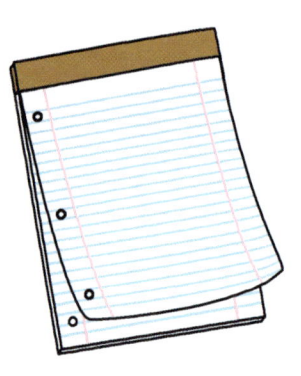

Arrange for your child to help care for a younger child. Have him plan how he will entertain the child by reading to him, helping him with homework, playing games with him, etc. If possible, take pictures of their time together. Then, ask your child to write about his experience, especially whether his planning was thorough enough to keep the younger child entertained.

Be Thorough

Parenting Activities

5. PHYSICAL
Be a Detective

These days, detective shows focus on investigators who are models of thoroughness. They don't miss a thing. Challenge your child to see which of you is the best detective. Go to a public place where you can sit down and watch people without being noticed. Parks and restaurants are good places. Decide on one person you will both watch for five minutes. From what you see, imagine the answers to the questions on page 77. When you are finished, compare notes. Who was the more thorough observer?

6. READING
Overcoming Challenges

In *Circle of Gold*, by Candy Dawson Boyd, Matti experiences one challenge after another in her quest for family healing after the death of her father. She strives hard to overcome each challenge, never giving up. Talk with your child about the good, and not so good, decisions Matti made.

Parenting Activities

Be Thorough

7. COMMUNITY
Learning from Katrina

Remember all the problems the city of New Orleans had during *Hurricane Katrina*? Some could not be avoided, but others happened because the people in charge were not thorough. They didn't anticipate problems, gather and use available resources together, take advantage of opportunities, or ask for help early enough. How prepared for an emergency are leaders of your community? Help your child investigate this question. You might get information from the mayor, city council, town planner, office of emergency preparedness, or fire department. If you think they need to be more prepared, your child can write them a letter and make some suggestions.

Positive Parenting Practices

Reward your child when he has been really thorough in completing a task. Make a list of privileges he can choose from when he has done a thorough job.

Be Thorough

Enrichment Activity

Activity 1: Physical—What Do You See?

Use the checklist below for the *Physical Activity* on page 75.

See how much you can tell about a person by observing him thoroughly for five minutes. No talking to the person and remember not to stare. You can circle things on the list below and write down words to help you remember the details when your five minutes are up.

How old is the person?

Married or single?

Rich, comfortable, or poor?

Happy or sad?

Energetic or not?

Children? How many?

What kind of house does this person live in?

What does this person like (reading, sports, art, music, etc.)?

Happy childhood or unhappy childhood?

What kind of job does this person have?

Where might this person have grown up (county, city, suburbs, etc.)?

What kind of future does this person have?

Be Thorough

Enrichment Activity

Activity 2: Project-Homework Help

A national survey showed that 68% of 4th graders are reading below grade level. One reason for that is that the way lessons are taught in school does not match the way some children learn. For instance, some children actually concentrate better when they are slouched in an easy chair with music in the background. Have your child review the list below and circle what works best for him. It will tell you some of the conditions that will actually make it easier for him to concentrate. For more information on learning styles, search "learning styles" on-line and ask your child's teacher.

Quiet	Cool Room	Lots of space around me
At a desk or table	Music playing	Doing homework after dinner
Spoken directions	Nobody around	Moving around every few minutes
No distractions	Snacks	Facing a wall
Warm room	Taking breaks	Talking about what I'm studying
Bright light	Reading	Soft chair
Sitting still	Writing things down	Doodling on the paper
Picturing something in my head	Studying in the morning	Answering questions
Written directions	Shady room	Listening

The circled words should give you clues on how to help your child study. Use these clues to help plan the best time of day to study and for how long at one time; the furniture, lighting, and noise level that help him concentrate; and whether to have people around or not.

There are several things that all children need, regardless of their learning style: water every 30 minutes or so; study material such as paper, pens, dictionary, etc.; clear understanding of the assignment; help only when necessary.

Be Thorough

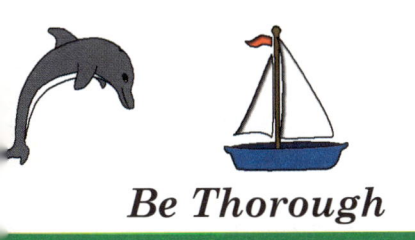

Enrichment Activity

Activity 3: Art–Brush Your Teeth Thoroughly

It's important to do a thorough job of brushing your teeth in order to prevent decay or gum disease. Have your child create a poster describing and/or listing the steps children need to follow to take care of their teeth. If this is something that your child needs to do better, put the poster in the bathroom.

- *Place the bristles of the toothbrush at an angle to your gums and make small circles over each tooth.*

- *Plaque and bacteria can collect where your gums meet your teeth, so remember to brush this area.*

- *Carefully brush the back and front of each tooth, then brush the chewing surfaces.*

- *Gently brush your gums to help prevent gum disease.*

- *Brush your tongue to remove bacteria, which will help to keep your breath fresh.*

- *Brush in front of a mirror so you can see what you are doing.*

Be Thorough

Enrichment Activity

Activity 4: Project—Thoroughness

Ask you child to circle all of the words below that have two E's in them. Afterward, check to see if he circled all of them. Discuss the importance of being thorough.

Education

Eager

Helper

Success

Grateful

President

Achievement

Thinker

Leader

Exceed

Vision

Enrichment

Gifted

Behave

Excitement

Active

Be Thorough

Positive Message

JULY

Activity 5: Visual Learning

Discuss with your child the positive message below. Post the message in a visible location for your child to see it often during the month. At the end of the month, complete *Activity 6* on the other side of this sheet.

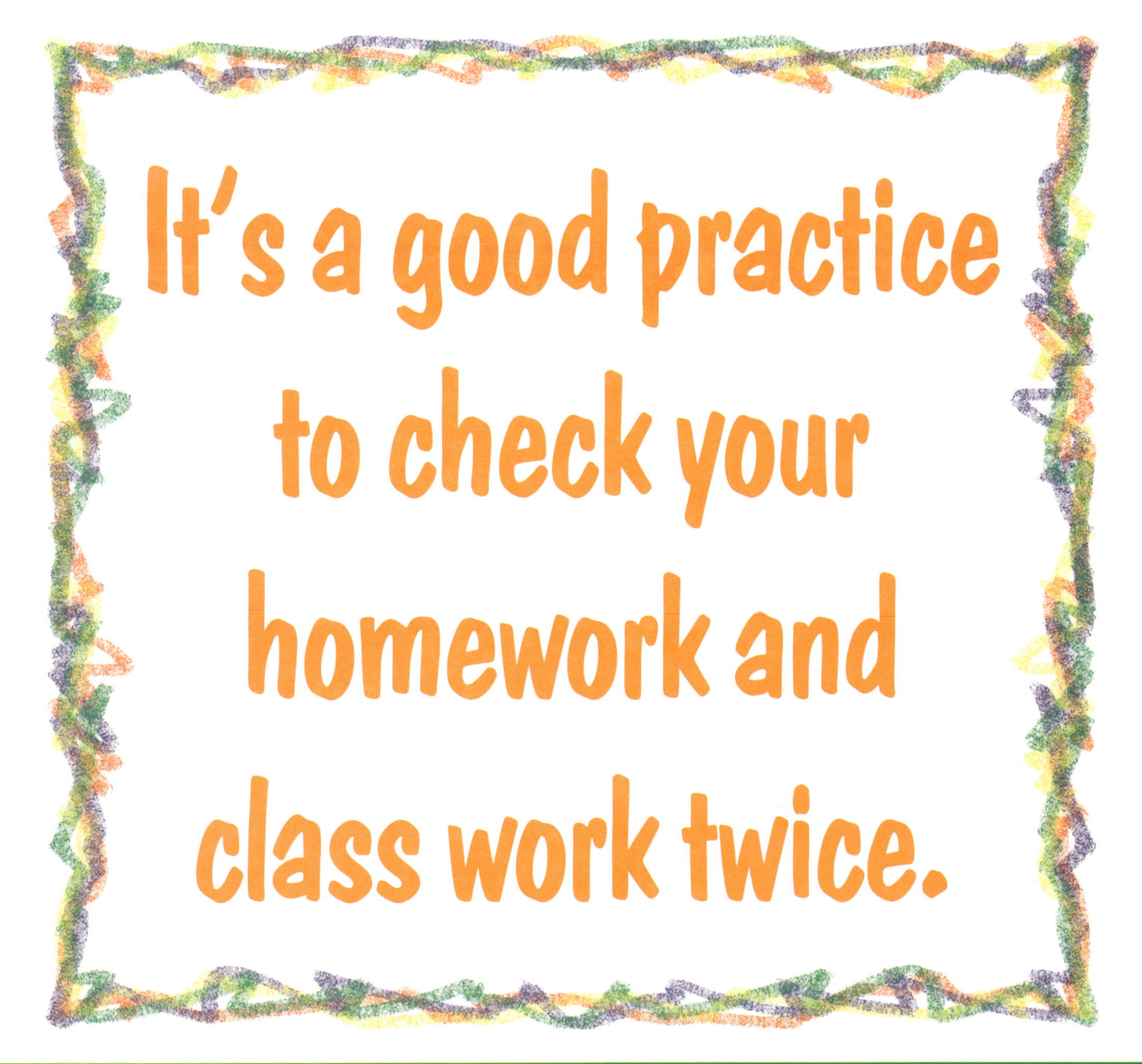

It's a good practice to check your homework and class work twice.

Be Thorough

Reinforcement Activity

Activity 6: I Am Thorough When . . .

Record examples of when your child was thorough and post in a visible location.

1. _____

2. _____

3. _____

4. _____

5. _____

Be Thorough

Reflection Activity

July

Activity 7: Reflection Log

Summarize your child's positive interactions during the month and reward yourself for a job well done.

Child's Name _____ **Date** _____

Name of Parent(s) _____

Record the number for each of the following questions in the box on the right.

A. How many of the workbook activities did you do with your child? ☐

B. How many positive recognitions did your child receive from teacher(s)? ☐

C. How many positive recognitions did your child receive from family members, friends, etc.? ☐

D. How many positive recognitions did your child receive from you, the parent(s)? ☐

Be Thorough

D. Record five self–initiated positive activities you did with your child that were not in this month's workbook activities.

1. _____

_____

2. _____

_____

3. _____

_____

4. _____

_____

5. _____

_____

The Value of Thriftiness

Parenting Activities

August

Message to Parents

Thriftiness is not just saving money here and there, it is a way of life that says "I value what I have and I won't waste it." This attitude should apply to all our resources.

1. COMMUNICATION
Value

The ease with which Americans can borrow money and buy what they want has led to a throw-away society. One study found that a family in France can live on what a similar family in America throws away. Establish an ongoing dialogue with your child about the value of money and the difference between what you want and what you need. Help your child keep track of her spending for the month and whether it was thoughtful and planned or impulsive. At the end of the month, was the impulse spending worth the cost?

2. ROLE PLAYING
Model It

The way you spend money, use your time, and take care of what you own sends a message about what you value in life. Show a healthy respect for money, make sure you compare prices when you shop, and stress the importance of saving for unexpected expenses. Parents need to explain where that cash comes from so that children don't grow to see ATM's as magical money machines. Make sure that all adults in the household are in agreement about how money is budgeted and spent.

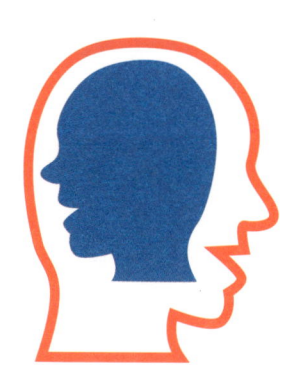

August

The Value of Thriftiness

Parenting Activities

3. TABLE TALK
Talk About It

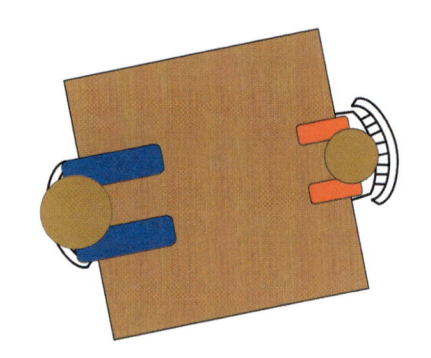

Discuss the following with your child:
- Buy cheap and you buy twice.
- Waste not, want not.
- Money is something I can always get again, time is gone forever.
- *Ask your child to tell you what she thinks you value most in life. Do your spending habits influence her response? Is that good or bad?*

4. WRITING
What Do You Want?

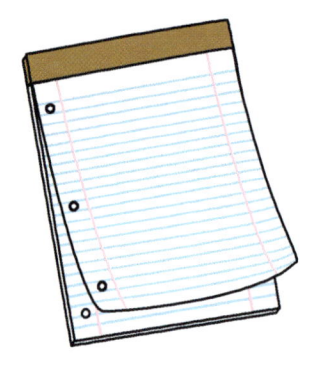

Goals can be a strong motivator to save money. Talk with your child about some of the things she would like to have now and in the future. Encourage her to make a folder in which she can keep pictures of items she wants and a list of written goals. She can add pictures and ideas over time. To get her started, have her write out what her long–term goals are and why they are important. Use pages 89 & 90 for writing.

The Value of Thriftiness

Parenting Activities

August

5. PHYSICAL

Budget

Give your child the experience of buying while using a budget. Have her plan a family meal on a budget of $10. Help her make a list of everything she needs for the meal. When you go to the store, take a calculator and keep track of the cost of each item. If she goes over budget, and she probably will, ask her to revise her menu. She may have to make several revisions. If you have a large family, you may want to increase her budget slightly.

6. READING

Using Ingenuity

The Boxcar Children, by Gertrude Chandler Warner, was first published over sixty years ago. It tells the tale of four orphans trying to escape being placed in a children's home. As you read it with your child, you can enjoy pointing out what life was like in decades past, and how the children used their ingenuity to find shelter and food, as well as learning how to get along.

Copyright© 2006 "I Care" Products & Services   (4th Grade)

Do Not Photocopy.

August

The Value of Thriftiness

Parenting Activities

7. COMMUNITY
Take It to the Bank

Help your child begin saving. Agree on what the savings will be used for and how much she will save from her allowance and from gifts of money. Before going to the bank, go to www.kidsbank.com and learn about banks, savings, interest, checks, and more. Ask your child to write down any questions she would like to ask the bank representative. While you are at the bank, encourage her to do the talking. Then, give her the responsibility for her savings book. You may also want to look into a certificate of deposit, savings bond, money market, or mutual funds.

Positive Parenting Practices

How often do you use money or "stuff" as a bribe to get your child to cooperate with you? Every parent has done it. They have bought a toy or candy just to quiet their child. However, once you start this, the precedent is hard to break. Instead, you should explain to your child that she can use her own money to save up for the desired item. You will be surprised how quickly interest can wane when children have to use their own money.

Do Not Photocopy.   Copyright© 2006 "I Care" Products & Services   (4th Grade)

The Value of Thriftiness

Enrichment Activity

Activity 1: Writing–Saving for the Future

Use the lines below for the *Writing Activity* on page 86.

August

The Value of Thriftiness

Enrichment Activity

The Value of Thriftiness

August

Activity 2: Project—Money Q & A

Introduce your child to www.zillions.org. This excellent website features *Consumer Reports 4 Kids* and has links where kids are advising kids about money matters (link to "Money Smarts", then to "Money Q & A"). Explore this site with your child. Then, ask her to put on her "Financial Advisor Visor" and answer the questions below.

Imagine you are a financial advisor for your friends. How would you answer the following questions?

1. I have a friend who borrows money and never pays me back. What should I do?

2. My mom said I could earn extra money by baby-sitting my little sister, but if I do, I won't be able to play with my friends after school. What do you suggest?

3. Help! I can't get everything I want with my allowance!

4. How can I get my parents to raise my allowance?

5. My parents are after me to save my money. How can I convince them I don't need to save?

Enrichment Activity

The Value of Thriftiness

Activity 3: Art—Make Your Own Bank

Everyone needs a place to stash cash. Talk with your child about the kind of bank she would like to make. Help your child create her own bank by following the directions below for *Decoupage*.

Decoupage

Decoupage is a way of decorating by cutting out pictures and pasting them to a surface in a creative way, then putting varnish over the top for protection. Here's what you do:

1. Use a clean container with a lid that you can cut a slit in.
2. Measure a piece of thick paper* that will wrap around the container.
3. Decorate the paper with paints, markers, or crayons. Be creative!
4. Cover the back of the paper with decoupage glue from the craft store and wrap the paper around the container.
5. To protect the bank, paint over the paper with one coat of the decoupage glue.

* Instead of using one large piece of paper, you could cut out small pictures and glue them one at a time over the surface of the container until the container is completely covered.

For more ideas, go to www.enchantedlearning.com and search for "piggy bank."

The Value of Thriftiness

Positive Message

August

Activity 4: Visual Learning

Discuss with your child the positive message below. Post the message in a visible location for your child to see it often during the month. At the end of the month, complete *Activity 5* on the other side of this sheet.

Use your time and money wisely.

The Value of Thriftiness

Reinforcement Activity

Activity 5: Understanding Thriftiness

Record some times your child demonstrated thriftiness and post in a visible location.

1. _____

2. _____

3. _____

4. _____

5. _____

The Value of Thriftness

Reflection Activity

August

Activity 6: Reflection Log

Summarize your child's positive interactions during the month and reward yourself for a job well done.

Child's Name _____ **Date** _____

Name of Parent(s) _____

Record the number for each of the following questions in the box on the right.

A. How many of the workbook activities did you do with your child? ☐

B. How many positive recognitions did your child receive from teacher(s)? ☐

C. How many positive recognitions did your child receive from family members, friends, etc.? ☐

D. How many positive recognitions did your child receive from you, the parent(s)? ☐

Copyright© 2006 "I Care" Products & Services   (4th Grade)   Do Not Photocopy.

August

The Value of Thriftiness

D. Record five self–initiated positive activities you did with your child that were not in this month's workbook activities.

1. _____
   _____

2. _____
   _____

3. _____
   _____

4. _____
   _____

5. _____
   _____

Be Creative Through Reading

Parenting Activities

Message to Parents

Children show a lot of creativity as they begin exploring the world. Too often, the routine of school and daily living teaches them to seek one right answer. You can help your child best by maintaining an environment and attitude that will protect and nurture creativity.

1. COMMUNICATION
Imagine That

The *9/11 Commission* concluded that "the most important failure" leading to the terrorist attacks "was one of imagination." That shows us the importance of creative thinking. The kind of imagination the *Commission* was talking about is looking for ways to improve something, even though it may seem fine the way it is, as well as an ability to accept change. On pages 101 and 102, you will find some ideas for increasing your child's creativity. Try them out.

2. ROLE PLAYING
Model It

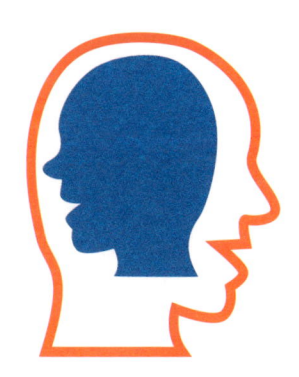

You may be more creative than you think. But, in case you doubt it, you can talk about other people who are creative. Get biographies of creative people from the library to read with your child. Some examples are Margaret Knight (the female Edison), Elijah McCoy (the "real McCoy"), or Benjamin Banneker (the African–American astronomer). You could also check out www.amazingkids.com and link to "Amazing Kids," where you can find some great examples of creativity.

Be Creative Through Reading

Parenting Activities

3. TABLE TALK
Talk About It

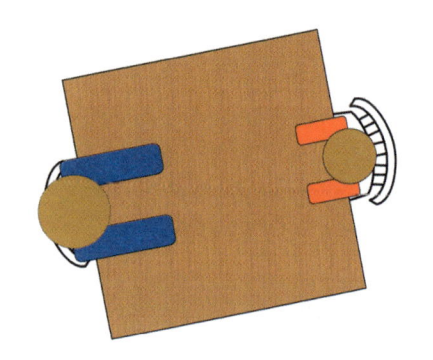

Discuss the following with your child:
- *"Whether you believe you can, or whether you believe you can't, you're absolutely right."*—Henry Ford
- *"Computers are useless. They can only give you answers."*—Pablo Picasso

4. WRITING
Let the Story Begin

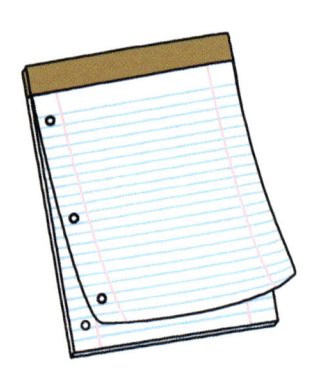

Have your child select a favorite story and create a description of what might have happened to the characters leading up to when the story begins. Encourage him to share his "prequel" with his class at school.

Be Creative Through Reading

Parenting Activities

5. PHYSICAL
Create a Dance

Have your child create a new dance that doesn't look like any that he's seen before. Have him give it a name. Talk about how he thought it up. Encourage him to teach it to his friends. That's one way that new fads catch on. Someone just started doing it.

6. READING
Anyone Can Do It

The Art Lesson, by Tomie dePaola, is actually intended for children between 4 and 8 years of age. However, the message it sends about creativity is so strong that anyone can appreciate it. Read over this book with your child. Then, have him read the book to a younger child. Talk about some of the things he might tell the youngster.

September — **Be Creative Through Reading**

Parenting Activities

7. COMMUNITY
Go Exploring

Explore with your child some of the opportunities in your community for developing creative expression. Painting, ceramics, jewelry making, creative writing, book making, video, weaving, poetry, and dancing are a few possibilities. If your child is interested, ask if you can visit a class. Let him try several until he finds one he'd like to pursue. The recreation center, the YMCA, and the library also have classes.

Positive Parenting Practices

Children who are rewarded for playing with toys stop playing with them once the reward is earned. Children who are not awarded for playing continue to play much longer.

100 — Do Not Photocopy. Copyright© 2006 "I Care" Products & Services (4th Grade)

Be Creative Through Reading

Enrichment Activity

Activity 1: Communication—Imagine That

One Right Answer or Lots of Possible Answers

Right answer thinking, also called convergent thinking, is important. But if that's all we do, we get stuck in a rut with no new ideas. To help your child develop the ability to also "think outside the box," to see new possibilities, and to come up with better answers, make a habit of asking "open" questions that have many possible answers. Below are some of the question starters you can use.

- **What if . . .**
- **How else might that have happened?**
- **How many ways can you use this?**
- **Name all the resources you could use.**
- **How many examples can you think of?**
- **What are your reasons for saying that?**
- **What are all the things that might happen?**
- **How else could you . . .**

Copyright© 2006 "I Care" Products & Services   (4th Grade)

Do Not Photocopy.

Be Creative Through Reading

Enrichment Activity

Brainstorming

If you need to get in the habit of asking "open" questions, try some brainstorming activities. Use the steps below to answer questions like "What are all the ways you could get home from school?"; "What would happen if there were no plastic?"; "What are all of the ways you can use a piece of string?"; etc. Once you are good at brainstorming, you can use it for all kinds of things, like listing all the things you need to do, recognizing all the consequences, thinking of the ways to accomplish a task, etc. It will improve your creativity.

Productive thinking is coming up with new, useful ideas. It's used in solving problems, making decisions, invention, and artistic creativity. We can improve our productive thinking by practicing several skills.

1. **Fluency**—Coming up with as many ideas as possible
2. **Flexibility**—Making the ideas different
3. **Elaboration**—Adding detail
4. **Originality**—Coming up with unique ideas

Fluency is having lots of ideas. We use brainstorming to help us be fluent.

Flexibility is being able to see things in a new way. Frisbees are an example of flexible thinking. Someone saw how kids were tossing around the pie tins from the Frisbee Pie Company after the pies were eaten and came up with the idea of tossing plastic discs. A multi–million dollar toy business was the result. The *Writing Activity* on page 26 and the *Art Activity* on page 30 practice flexibility.

Elaboration is adding lots of detail so that people understand an idea better. Poets use this by creating word pictures to express their feelings. Businesses do this in reports when they include pages of details to explain new policy. Clothing designers add and change details so there are always new fashions for the customer to buy. The *Art Activity* on page 30 is about elaboration.

Originality is having ideas that are unique or unusual. You recognize originality because the ideas, inventions, or art works are so different and not like those of anyone else. Picasso was considered original when he broke away from traditional painting. The airplane and automobile were original. You can practice originality with the project on page 41.

Reference: E. Paul Torrance, *The Search for Satori and Creativity* (1979).

Be Creative Through Reading

Enrichment Activity

Activity 2: Project-Haiku

Haiku is a form of poetry that began in Japan centuries ago. It seems very simple because it is so short, usually just three lines. Actually, it takes creative thinking to follow the rules of writing haiku and use so few words to say a lot. Read over the examples and rules of haiku below and try writing some haiku poems with your child. Copy your favorites to hang up. Share them with family and friends.

Rules for Haiku Poems

1. Three lines and a total of 17 syllables
   - Line one = 5 syllables
   - Line two = 7 syllables
   - Line three = 5 syllables
2. Words that describe something in nature or everyday life.
3. You can hear two parts as you read them. One part is a description and the other is a thought about it.

Getting Started:

Think of something simple you want to write about. Brainstorm a list of words that describe it. Then, begin combining the words in different ways to fit the rules of haiku.

Enrichment Activity

Be Creative Through Reading

Basho Matsuo, a famous Japanese haiku master, lived from 1644 to 1694. Below are two of his poems.

An old pond!
A frog jumps in—
The sound of water.

The first soft snow!
Enough to bend the leaves
Of the jonquil low.

Here are some haiku poems by children.

Sunshine: golden, warm,
Floating in the sky above.
It kisses my face.

Jaguar fleet of foot,
As fast as a forceful wind.
Symbol of freedom.

Now try some of your own!

_____   _____

_____   _____

_____   _____

_____   _____

_____   _____

Be Creative Through Reading

Activity 3: Art–Still Life

One aspect of creativity is the ability to see things from many points of view. Artists are good at this. The Impressionist painter Claude Monet painted a series of haystacks to show how the landscape changed, depending on the amount of light in the sky. Other artists would paint the same object using different colors, different kinds of paints, or different brush techniques. Others have painted the same object from different angles, so you see it from all sides. Some afternoon when you want to enjoy time with your child, create a still life (a collection of objects). Then, each of you paint five different pictures of the still life. Be creative by using different kinds of paints, different brush strokes, different colors, different angles, and anything else you can think of to make the paintings different from each other. Try to make each one different, but still represent the objects in the still life. Compare your pictures. Share them with family and friends. You don't have to be artistically talented to enjoy this activity.

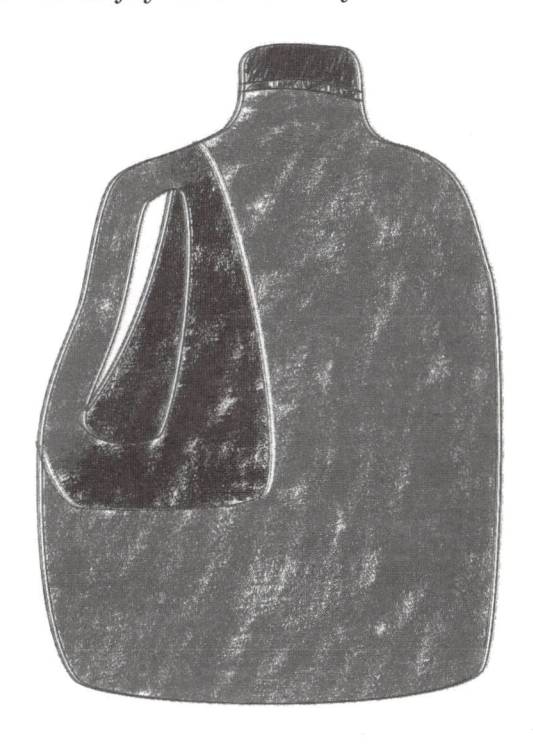

September

Be Creative Through Reading

Activity 4: Project-Making Reading Fun!

The start of the school year is an excellent time to make reading fun and to introduce your child to different types of reading sources. Discuss the value of the information provided in each source below.

Newspaper

Self-Help Magazine

Novel

Catalog

Science Book

Newsletter

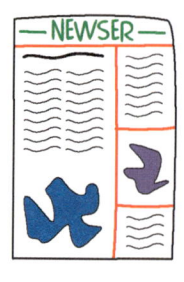

Workbook

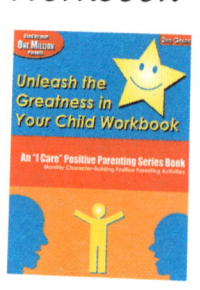

Text Book

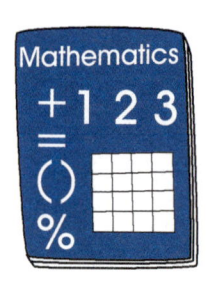

Sports Magazine

106
Do Not Photocopy.   Copyright© 2006 "I Care" Products & Services   (4th Grade)

Be Creative Through Reading

Positive Message

September

Activity 5: Visual Learning

Discuss with your child the positive message below. Post the message in a visible location for your child to see it often during the month. At the end of the month, complete *Activity 6* on the other side of this sheet.

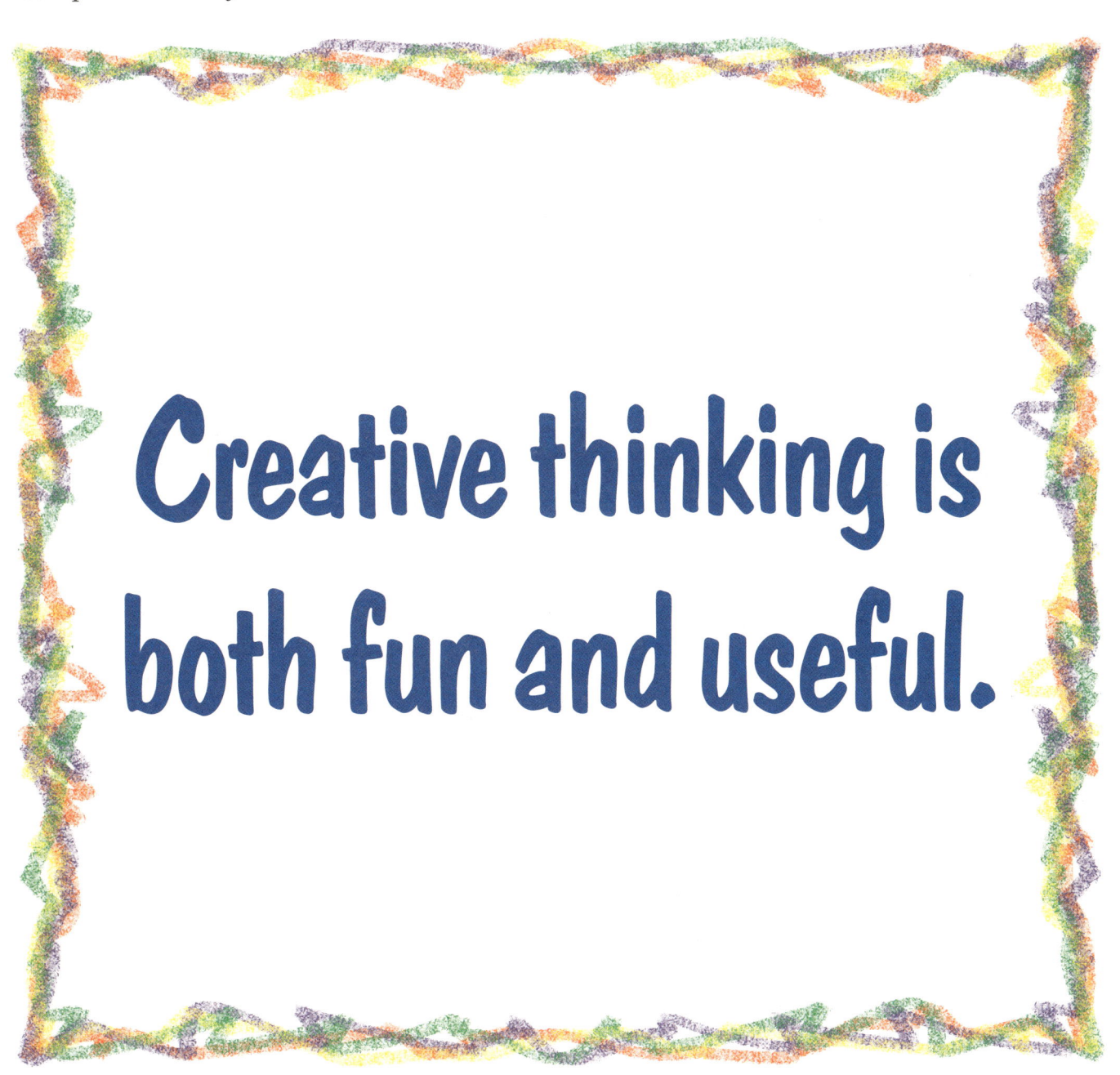

Creative thinking is both fun and useful.

Be Creative Through Reading

Reinforcement Activity

Activity 6: Being Creative Through Reading

Record some times your child was creative through reading and post in a visible location.

1. _____

2. _____

3. _____

4. _____

5. _____

Be Creative Through Reading

Reflection Activity

September

Activity 7: Reflection Log

Summarize your child's positive interactions during the month and reward yourself for a job well done.

Child's Name _____ Date _____

Name of Parent(s) _____

Record the number for each of the following questions in the box on the right.

A. How many of the workbook activities did you do with your child? ☐

B. How many positive recognitions did your child receive from teacher(s)? ☐

C. How many positive recognitions did your child receive from family members, friends, etc.? ☐

D. How many positive recognitions did your child receive from you, the parent(s)? ☐

Be Creative Through Reading

D. Record five self-initiated positive activities you did with your child that were not in this month's workbook activities.

1. _____

   _____

2. _____

   _____

3. _____

   _____

4. _____

   _____

5. _____

   _____

Be Joyful

October

Parenting Activities

Message to Parents

Joy is a recognition of what is good in life. It is being happy without reservation. Joy is a choice, an attitude, a way of seeing life that goes beyond our circumstances. Joyful children grow up to become well–adjusted adults.

1. COMMUNICATION
What Brings You Joy?

Fly Away Home is a movie about a 13–year–old girl building a relationship with her father after her mother's death. Against this background she nurtures a flock of orphaned geese, deciding to teach them to fly instead of clipping their wings. After watching the movie as a family, ask each person how his or her heart felt as the geese finally soared home. Talk about the kinds of things in your own lives that bring joy to your hearts.

2. ROLE PLAYING
Model It

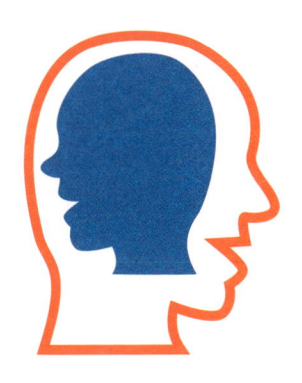

Is your joy bucket full or empty? When you wake up in the morning, are you looking forward to the day or dreading it? Do you enjoy your work, the people around you, and your family? If not, you're probably not a model of joy for your child. When circumstances make it difficult to laugh, look for the little things that are beautiful, funny, or cute and express your joy for them.

October

Be Joyful

Parenting Activities

3. TABLE TALK
Talk About It

Discuss the following with your child:
- What are some of the things that are interesting about you, that you are proud of?
- Tell me some of the things that make you happy. Why do they?
- "We could never learn to be brave and patient if there were only joy in the world."—Helen Keller, author who was deaf and blind.
- "A thing of beauty is a joy forever."—John Keats, poet.

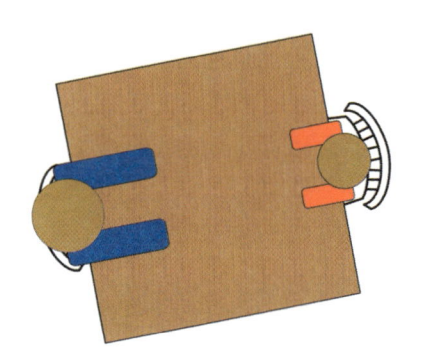

4. WRITING
Fun With Words

"Shape poems" not only tell about something, they show as well. Look at the example on page 115. See how the words of the poem about fish are arranged to create the shape of a fish. Make a list of as many words as you can that express joy. Create a shape poem out of them. Use the guide on page 115 to get started.

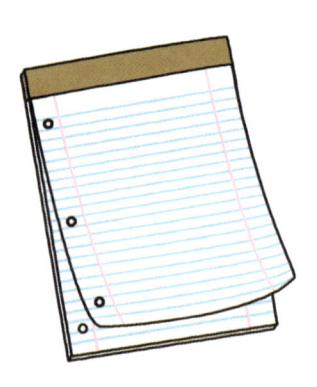

Do Not Photocopy. Copyright© 2006 "I Care" Products & Services (4th Grade)

Be Joyful

Parenting Activities

5. PHYSICAL
Laughter Is the Best Medicine

It's a fact that laughter may help prevent a heart attack. A study by the University of Maryland found that people with heart disease were 40 percent less likely to laugh in a variety of situations compared to people of the same age without heart disease. What do you laugh about? How about your child? One way to share a laugh is to watch the television show *America's Funniest Home Videos*. Laugh out loud! How do you feel afterward?

6. READING
Achievement

Justin and the Best Biscuits in the World, by Mildred Pitts Walter, tells the story of ten-year-old Justin who can't seem to do anything right until he spends the summer with Grandpa on his ranch. Read about Justin's adventures and talk about how little achievements can be really rewarding.

October

Be Joyful

Parenting Activities

7. COMMUNITY
Folk Art

Enjoy the last days of fall at a folk art fair. There's bound to be one near you. There are wonderful ways to introduce your child to a wide variety of artisans, regional music and foods, interesting crafts, and local history. Dialogue with her about her favorite experience. Did it spark a desire to learn a craft herself. If so, follow up.

Positive Parenting Practices

Show your child how much she is loved. Saying "I love you" seems like such a small thing, but it is really important. Make it a habit to tell your child how much you love her. Give her hugs, too.

Be Joyful

Enrichment Activity

October

Activity 1: Writing-Shape Poems

Use this page for the *Writing Activity* on page 112.

Shape poems are fun to create. See how simple it is to write a "Fish" poem? Create your own shape poem about something that brings you joy and makes you happy.

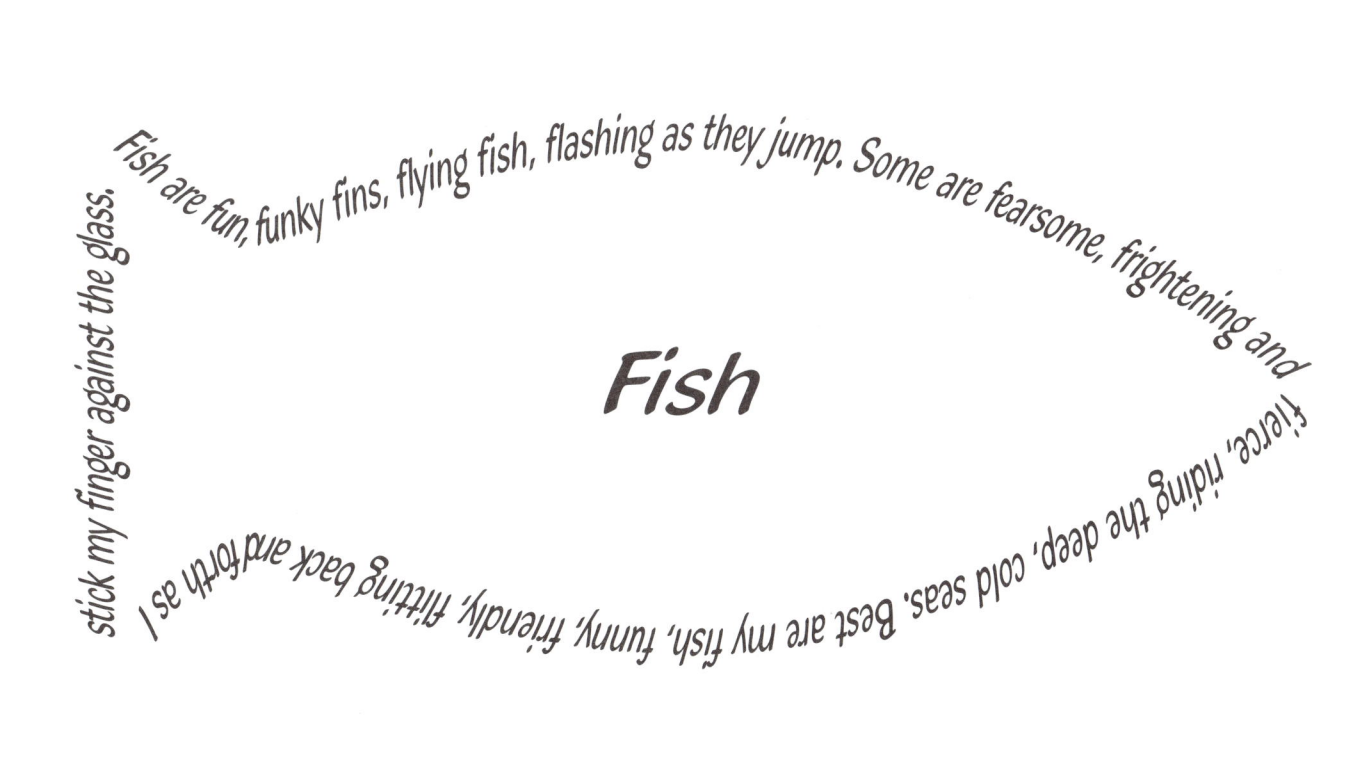

Fish are fun, funky fins, flying fish, flashing as they jump. Some are fearsome, frightening and fierce, riding the deep, cold seas. Best are my fish, funny, friendly, flitting back and forth as I stick my finger against the glass.

Fish

115

Copyright© 2006 "I Care" Products & Services (4th Grade)

Do Not Photocopy.

October

Be Joyful

Writing My Own Shape Poem

Something that brings me joy and makes me happy _____
_____.

Words to describe it: _____
_____
_____.

My shape poem:

Be Joyful

Enrichment Activity

Activity 2: Art—Having Fun With Idioms

Idioms are a part of our language, but when people from another country hears one, they don't have a clue what it means. Check out the idioms below. Make sure your child could explain them all. Then, have her select two of her favorites and draw a picture of the literal meaning.

Do you know what all of these phrases mean?

- An eager beaver
- Jump down someone's throat
- Elbow grease
- Raining cats and dogs
- Pulling your leg
- Bend over backwards
- Butterflies in the stomach
- Give someone a hand
- Go with the flow
- Feel like a million dollars
- Get off my back
- The cat's out of the bag
- Break the ice
- Have a ball
- Head over heels
- Head in the clouds
- Caught red-handed
- Cough it up

Be Joyful

Activity 3: Project–Tradition

Family traditions are ways of making the memories that will keep family alive in the life of your child as she grows older. What are some of the traditions in your family? Family night movie and pizza, reading every night before bed, having a block party every summer, kids cooking once a month, worshipping together as a family, and taking dinner to people who are shut–in are all good examples. As a family, decide on one more tradition you would like to establish. It can be as simple as taking turns selecting a topic to discuss at dinner to going camping in the winter. Then, do it!

Be Joyful

Enrichment Activity

October

Activity 4: Art–Pat on the Back

Give your child "Pat–on–the–back" awards often. Cut out the hand below and trace it onto construction paper. Cut out the traced hand and tape the two hands together. When your child does something well, give her a pat on the back. Encourage other family members to also give pats–on–the–back.

Copyright© 2006 "I Care" Products & Services   (4th Grade)

Do Not Photocopy.

119

October

Be Joyful

Cut out the hand template on the other side of this page for the Art Activity.

Be Joyful

Positive Message

October

Activity 4: Visual Learning

Discuss with your child the positive message below. Post the message in a visible location for your child to see it often during the month. At the end of the month, complete *Activity 5* on the other side of this sheet.

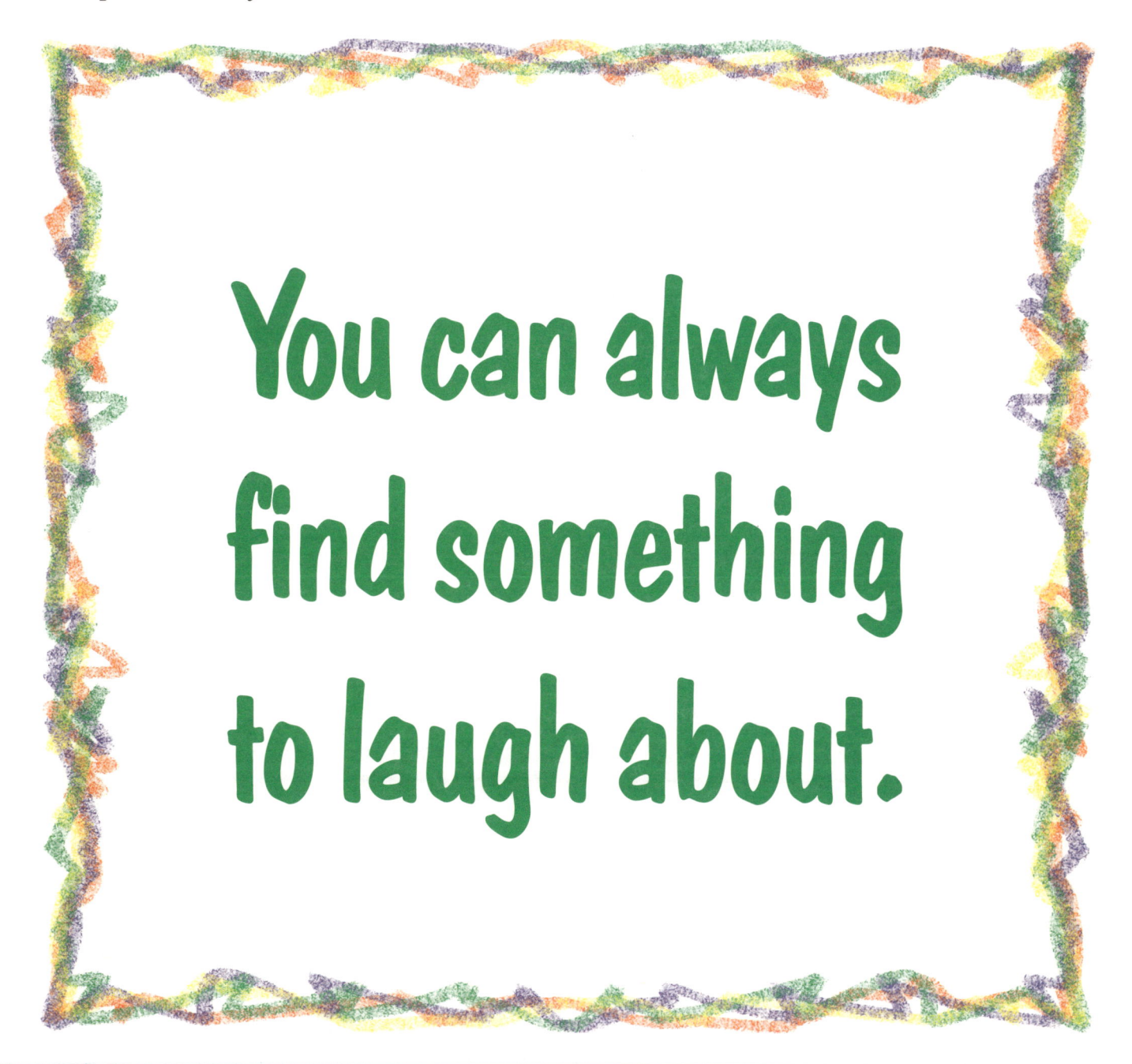

You can always find something to laugh about.

October

Be Joyful

Reinforcement Activity

Activity 5: Being Joyful

Record some joyful times you've shared with your child and post in a visible location.

1. _____

2. _____

3. _____

4. _____

5. _____

Be Joyful

Reflection Activity

October

Activity 6: Reflection Log

Summarize your child's positive interactions during the month and reward yourself for a job well done.

Child's Name _____ **Date** _____

Name of Parent(s) _____

Record the number for each of the following questions in the box on the right.

A. How many of the workbook activities did you do with your child? ☐

B. How many positive recognitions did your child receive from teacher(s)? ☐

C. How many positive recognitions did your child receive from family members, friends, etc.? ☐

D. How many positive recognitions did your child receive from you, the parent(s)? ☐

Copyright© 2006 "I Care" Products & Services   (4th Grade)   Do Not Photocopy.

October

Be Joyful

D. Record five self–initiated positive activities you did with your child that were not in this month's workbook activities.

1. _____

_____

2. _____

_____

3. _____

_____

4. _____

_____

5. _____

_____

Have Honor

Parenting Activities

November

Message to Parents

Honor is a little more than being polite. It also implies having great respect for someone and standing up for what you believe to be right.

1. COMMUNICATION
Kinds of Honor

Our concept of honor has changed greatly over time. When the United States was founded, honor was considered a kind of "nobility of the soul" that originated in the actions of the person who had it. Today, the emphasis placed on personal freedom and doing things your own way leaves little room for a common standard of honor. On page 129, you will find a list of different kinds of honor. As you go over each one, your child's understanding of honor will expand.

2. ROLE PLAYING
Model It

Emphasize one courteous act a week. Talk about it and practice it with your child. Begin with being polite to one another, following through when you say you will do something, communicating better, being on time, and listening well. These are ways to honor one another.

Copyright© 2006 "I Care" Products & Services (4th Grade)

Do Not Photocopy.

November

Have Honor

Parenting Activities

3. TABLE TALK

Talk About It

Discuss the following with your child:
- What are some of the ways you can show honor to your teacher?
- Two hundred years ago, men were willing to fight a duel to the death with anyone who even questioned their honor. (Alexander Hamilton, the man whose face is on the ten dollar bill, was killed in a duel with Aaron Burr, who was Vice President of the United States at the time.) Why do you think they had a duel? Do some research to find out why.

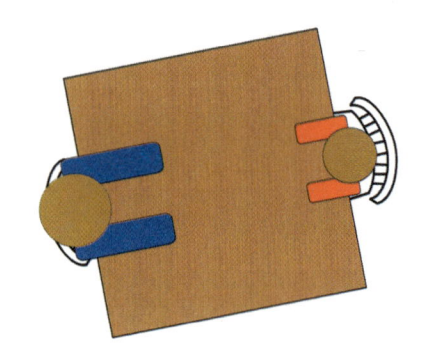

4. WRITING

Honor Code

Many schools use honor codes to emphasize the importance of honor. In some, when you break the honor code, you must go before the honor court to defend your behavior. In others, the code is meant to make behavior expectations clear. As a family, discuss the honorable behaviors that you want to uphold. Then, ask your child to create a code of honor, a document that you can post and refer to that will remind everyone of the behavior standards. See page 130 for a sample honor code.

Have Honor

Parenting Activities

November

5. PHYSICAL
Show Honor

Have your child practice appropriate ways to show honor in the following situations: someone gives him a gift; he accidentally bumps into someone; he meets an important person for the first time; a friend's pet has just died.

6. READING
Winning Hearts

Sarah, Plain and Tall, by Patricia MacLachlan, was so popular that it was eventually made into a made-for-TV movie. After enjoying the book, see if you can rent the movie. Talk about how Sarah won the hearts of Anna and Caleb, and how they eventually came to honor her.

November

Have Honor

Parenting Activities

7. COMMUNITY
Good Samaritan Award

Most public servants deserve our honor and recognition. Writing letters of commendation or letters to the editor, calling someone's boss, making an award certificate for someone, giving someone a party, defending someone when another person criticizes him, and baking someone cookies are just a few examples of recognition. Help your child identify someone in your community who has gone out of his or her way to help others and honor them in one of the ways mentioned above.

Positive Parenting Practices

Catch your child showing honor and acknowledge it.

128
Do Not Photocopy.   Copyright© 2006 "I Care" Products & Services   (4th Grade)

Have Honor

Enrichment Activity

November

Activity 1: Communication–Kinds of Honor

Use the list below for the *Communication Activity* on page 125.

- Honor Roll
- Honor Society
- Honor Code
- Word of Honor
- Affairs of Honor (Fighting a Duel)
- Taking Honors (Signed Up for the Most Difficult Classes in School)
- Honor a Check
- Point of Honor
- Code of Honor
- Honor Bound
- An Honor to His Profession
- Medal of Honor
- Honorary Degree
- Pledge of Honor
- Honor Student
- Debt of Honor
- The Price of Honor
- Honor Guard
- On My Honor
- Her Honor, the Mayor
- Maid of Honor
- Matron of Honor
- Honor Court
- Dishonor
- I Have the Honor to Present
- Honors, High Honors (Top Grades)
- Word of Honor
- Your Honor (To a Judge)
- Honor Ceremonies (Pow-Wows).

Enrichment Activity

Have Honor

Activity 2: Writing—Honor Codes

Use the fact sheet on this page for the *Writing Activity* on page 126.

Some honor codes are very simple, like the statement students make after a test:

> "I hereby declare, on my honor, that I have not given or received help from anyone or anything during this test."

Some honor codes are a list of do's and don'ts, like this code for a sports team:
- Winning first, team second, you third
- Support your teammates
- If you're called out, you're out
- Be on time
- Celebrate wins
- Be a good loser

For your family code of honor, you might want to include things like:
- Treat all people with respect
- Tell the truth

Some topics might be:
- Respect
- Truth
- Loyalty
- Patience
- Responsibility
- Being on time
- Forgiveness
- Sharing

Have Honor

Enrichment Activity

November

Activity 3: Art-Story Quilt

Faith Ringgold is a famous artist best known for her story quilts—a story told through pictures. Have your child create a story poster about honor in the style of Ringgold's quilts. He can create a story about children honoring their parents, different family members honoring each other, a country honoring its veterans, etc. Any story of honor is appropriate. The directions below will help him get started.

Materials: pencil, markers or paint, glue, construction paper, drawing paper, poster paper, scissors

Making a "Story Quilt" Poster

A story quilt is a story told through pictures, with some words added along the way. You can find wonderful examples at www.faithringgold.com (link to "Where you can see my art" and click on some of her story quilts). Notice how the artist used fabric, cut and sewn as pictures. You can simply draw the pictures and the drawing doesn't have to look perfect, just have enough detail.

You start a story quilt/poster with a story. Write down six major events that tell your story. Draw each scene, using the same sized paper for each. Add color and detail to make the pictures interesting and relate facts about the story.

Glue the pictures to the poster board in sequence. You may want to leave space between each for creating a decorative border, or even writing some dialogue of the characters, the moral of the story, or something about the story that you want to emphasize.

Give your quilt a title and add it to the quilt in some creative way, such as in the border, across the corner, or in a quote bubble next to someone's mouth.

To preserve this work of art, you may want to spray it with a fixative available at a craft store.

Have Honor

Activity 4: Project-By Proclamation

People are honored in many ways. People, places, and things are named after them. Book dedications, flowers, gifts, letters of appreciation, awards, and certificates are all given to honor people. Some people even have a special day dedicated to them by proclamation. Talk with your child about whom he might want to honor by proclamation. It could be a relative, a teacher, or even you. Have him create a certificate of proclamation to give to that person and plan a special recognition of the day of honor. Perhaps he can bake cookies for the person of honor.

Certificate of Proclamation

Presented to Mary White for her love for and devotion to her family. She is a constant joy in everyone's life.

Signed this day,

Johnny

Have Honor

Positive Message

November

Activity 5: Visual Learning

Discuss with your child the positive message below. Post the message in a visible location for your child to see it often during the month. At the end of the month, complete *Activity 6* on the other side of this sheet.

> I am honored when you say kind words like "I'm sorry," "Excuse me," "Thank you," and "Please."

Copyright© 2006 "I Care" Products & Services (4th Grade)

Do Not Photocopy.

November

Have Honor

Reinforcement Activity

Activity 6: Have Honor

Record times your child was recognized for special achievements and post in a visible location.

1. _____

2. _____

3. _____

4. _____

5. _____

134
Do Not Photocopy.   Copyright© 2006 "I Care" Products & Services   (4th Grade)

Have Honor

November

Reflection Activity

Activity 7: Reflection Log

Summarize your child's positive interactions during the month and reward yourself for a job well done.

Child's Name _____ **Date** _____

Name of Parent(s) _____

Record the number for each of the following questions in the box on the right.

A. How many of the workbook activities did you do with your child? ☐

B. How many positive recognitions did your child receive from teacher(s)? ☐

C. How many positive recognitions did your child receive from family members, friends, etc.? ☐

D. How many positive recognitions did your child receive from you, the parent(s)? ☐

November

Have Honor

D. Record five self–initiated positive activities you did with your child that were not in this month's workbook activities.

1. _____

   _____

2. _____

   _____

3. _____

   _____

4. _____

   _____

5. _____

   _____

Be Reliable

December

Parenting Activities

Message to Parents

It is necessary to be reliable in life. Reliability is most easily taught to young children by holding them accountable. In other words, they need to understand the connection between behavior and consequences.

1. COMMUNICATION
Consequences

Computers have revolutionized our world. We rely on them for almost everything we do. Talk with your child about what would happen if there were a computer malfunction in a bank, a hospital, a store, or a school. It may help her to understand that there are always consequences when the things or people we are depending on are not reliable.

2. ROLE PLAYING
Model It

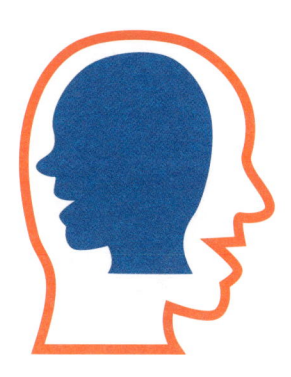

Your child will only be as reliable as you are. That's what the research says. If you're having trouble teaching your child to follow through on responsibility, do a self–check. Do you keep your word? Are you home when you say you will be there? Can people count on you? If not, you may want to make some changes.

December

Be Reliable

Parenting Activities

3. TABLE TALK

Talk About It

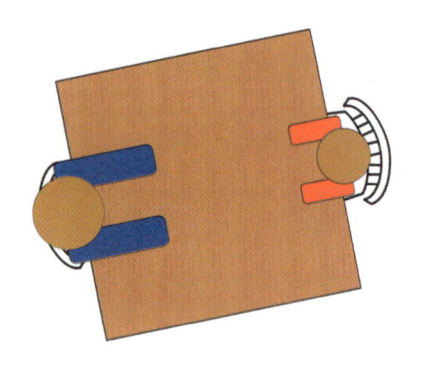

Discuss the following with your child:
- If you make excuses all of the time for why you can't get something done, people will start to think that you're unreliable. What would be some legitimate excuses for not doing your homework?
- What would happen if the school bus did not follow the same route every day?
- It's better to be early than to be late.

4. WRITING

Vote for Me

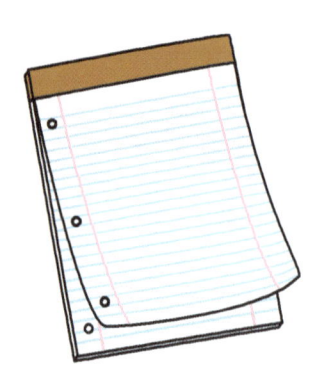

Class officers have to be reliable. Have your child write a speech to convince her classmates to vote for her as class president or some other officer. She should emphasize some ways that she is reliable.

Be Reliable

Parenting Activities

5. PHYSICAL
In Case of Emergency

In an emergency, it's important to have reliable people around. Feeling prepared and knowing what to do will enable your child to stay calm and act reliably. On page 141, you will find some hints for being prepared in case of an emergency. Go over these with your child.

6. READING
Overcoming Fear

The Courage of Sarah Noble, by Alice Dalgliesh, tells the true story of a young girl on the American frontier of 1707 and how she conquered fear and the unknown. Have your child imagine along with you what Sarah was really feeling, especially when she was alone with an Indian family for weeks.

Be Reliable

Parenting Activities

7. COMMUNITY

Fast Food

We often make assumptions that business and government do things for the public good. That's not always true—profit is another motive. Scientists are telling us that we have become a fat nation. Everyone is overweight. What is to blame? We watch TV and sit at our computers. We ride instead of walking. We eat fast food. How reliable are the ads that we see and hear?

Positive Parenting Practices

Never nag. If your child fails to follow through, impose natural consequences. Example: "You can't go to the movie because your chores aren't done."

Be Reliable

Enrichment Activity — December

Activity 1: Physical–In Case of Emergency

Use this fact sheet for the *Physical Activity* on page 139.

Even with all the warnings we hear in the media, most people will probably never have to live through disaster. But, it's always good to be prepared. The following suggestions come from FEMA (Federal Emergency Management Agency, www.fema.gov).

Do you know what kinds of disasters might happen where you live?
You can find out by going to www.fema.gov/kids.

Does your family have a disaster kit?
There are basic supplies that can be used in any disaster. They include the following:
- **Water**—a gallon a day per person for at least 3 days.
- **Food**—canned meats, soup, and fruit; high energy food like peanut butter, jelly, crackers, granola bars, etc.; hard candy; special food for babies or older people.
- **Clothes**—one complete change of clothes; sturdy, water-proof shoes; rain gear for everyone; sleeping bags or blankets.
- **Tools and First Aid Supplies**—there are lots of things that would be helpful. If you go to www.redcross.org, you'll find a good list. You can also call your local *Red Cross*.

What will you do if everyone has to evacuate?
Make plans about what to do in each of the following situations:
- If something happens to your home, where will everyone meet? Could you meet at the home of a neighbor? A store down the road or some other public place?
- If you must leave your neighborhood, where will everyone meet? The home of a friend or relative would be a good choice.
- How can you find each other if you become separated? Everyone should memorize the phone number of a relative who lives in another state, or, at the very least, in another part of the state. You can call there to tell them where you are located.

Be Reliable

Activity 2: Art—"Yellow Pages" Ad

How many of us rely on what we hear in commercials or read in ads when we are considering making a purchase or contracting a service? Advertisers count on ads and word them in such a way as to appeal to the wants and needs of customers. Have your child create a "yellow pages" ad that advertises a product or a service. Talk with her about what the customer would want to know and how she could emphasize the company's reliability. Encourage her to be creative. If she makes an ad for a local store or service, see if she wants to give it to them. They may want to use it.

Be Reliable

Enrichment Activity

Activity 3: Project-Helping Caregivers

Children rely on their parents to care for them as they learn to care for themselves. That's part of life. Then, as parents become senior citizens, they rely on their children. This is happening more and more as the number of senior citizens in this country increases. The adult children who take care of their elderly parents are called *caregivers* and they have a big job with not a lot of help. Caregivers are also the people who take care of the sick and disabled, no matter how old they are. Below, you will find some suggestions on how to lighten the load of a caregiver that you might know. Review the list with your child and select one or more activities the two of you can do this month.

A caregiver must always be reliable. Sometimes, that can be hard. Select someone you know who is a caregiver. Make a project of helping that person throughout the month to show your appreciation.

- Let the caregiver know that no one will judge him badly for taking time for himself.
- Fix a special meal and take it to the person.
- Go shopping for groceries or run errands for the person.
- Do laundry for the person for one week.
- Offer to sit with the person being cared for so the caregiver can take a day off, or raise money to hire a trained person to care for someone who requires special care.
- Introduce the caregiver to someone else who is or has been a caregiver.
- Help the caregiver find support. If he needs support that you can't give, make a few phone calls to find a community resource that he can turn to for support.
- Make an "I Care" kit. Caregivers don't have much time for themselves, so they would appreciate a little pampering. The kit could include healthy snacks, DVD's, microwave popcorn, and books on tape.

Be Reliable

Enrichment Activity

Activity 4: Project-Always on Time

Establish rewards for your child to complete tasks on time. Use encouraging phrases often to reward desired behaviors. Examples could be "I'm proud of you"; "You met my expectation"; "Thanks for being on time"; etc.

Establish your rewards for the following:

On Time Actions	Reward
• Taking out the garbage	_____
• Completing homework	_____
• Getting home after school on time	_____
• Making good grades	_____
• Limiting T.V. watching	_____
• Cleaning room	_____

Be Reliable

December

Positive Message

Activity 4: Visual Learning

Discuss with your child the positive message below. Post the message in a visible location for your child to see it often during the month. At the end of the month, complete *Activity 5* on the other side of this sheet.

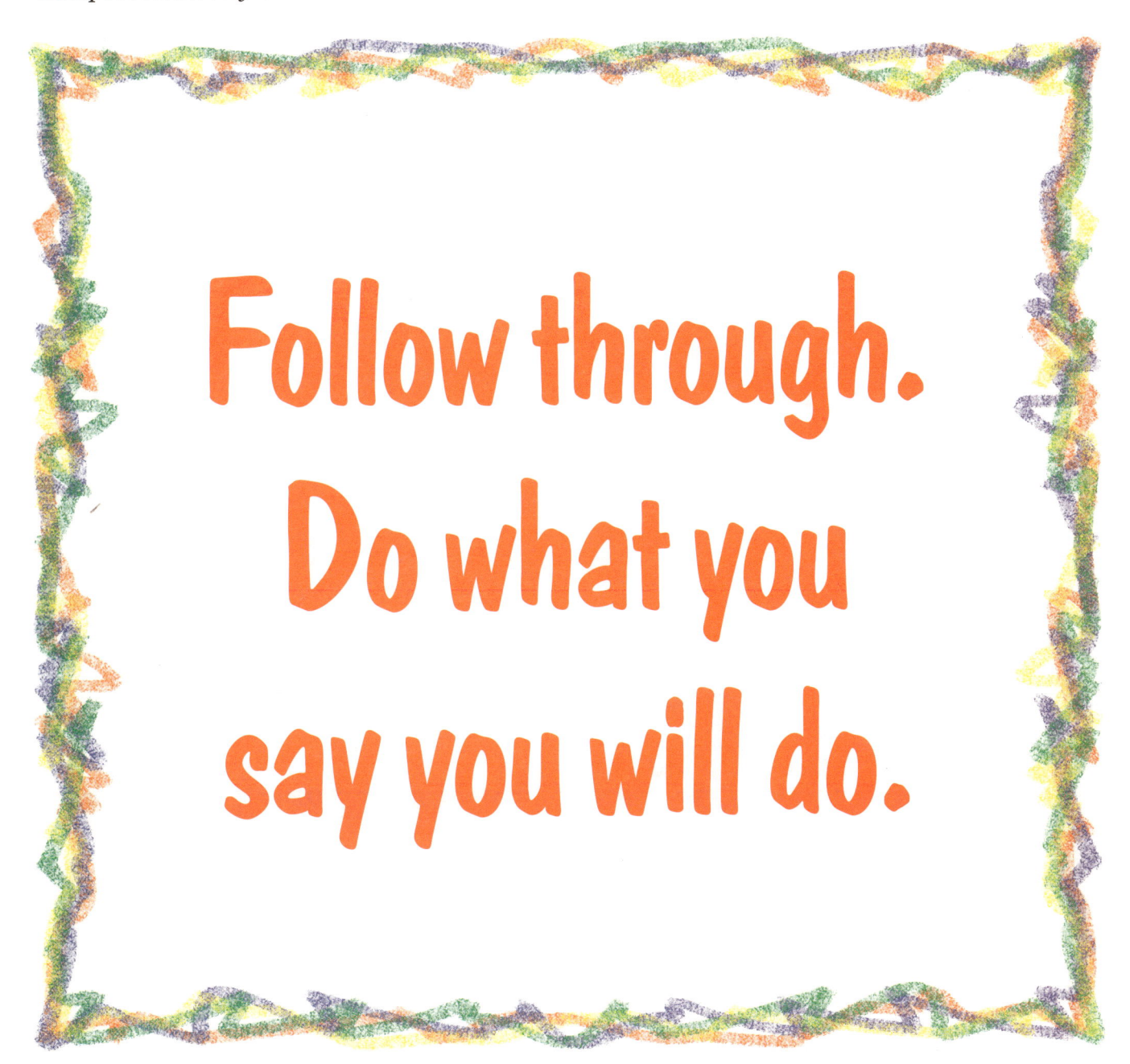

Follow through. Do what you say you will do.

December

Be Reliable

Reinforcement Activity

Activity 5: Be Reliable

Record times when your child was reliable and post in a visible location.

1. _____

2. _____

3. _____

4. _____

5. _____

Be Reliable

December

Reflection Activity

Activity 6: Reflection Log

Summarize your child's positive interactions during the month and reward yourself for a job well done.

Child's Name _____ **Date** _____

Name of Parent(s) _____

Record the number for each of the following questions in the box on the right.

A. How many of the workbook activities did you do with your child? ☐

B. How many positive recognitions did your child receive from teacher(s)? ☐

C. How many positive recognitions did your child receive from family members, friends, etc.? ☐

D. How many positive recognitions did your child receive from you, the parent(s)? ☐

Copyright© 2006 "I Care" Products & Services (4th Grade)

Do Not Photocopy.

December

Be Reliable

D. Record five self-initiated positive activities you did with your child that were not in this month's workbook activities.

1. _____
   _____

2. _____
   _____

3. _____
   _____

4. _____
   _____

5. _____
   _____

Recommended Books

To order a set of books that corresponds to the Positive Parenting Activities in this Workbook, or to order additional Workbooks from the "Unleash the Greatness in Your Child" Series or "I Care" books (see following pages), fill out the order form below. Then, cut the form along the dotted line and tear out the card along the perforation. Send the card along with check, money order, or credit card information in an envelope and mail it to the address shown on the card. You can also place your order at www.icarenow.com/parents.html, or e–mail the information requested on the card to parents7@icarenow.com.

4th Grade Book Pack $51.95

Art Lesson, The
Boxcar Children, The
Caleb's Story
Circle of Gold
Courage of Sarah Noble, The
Egg Drop Blues
Hundred Penny Box, The
Justin and the Best Biscuits in the World
Sadako and the Thousand Paper Cranes
Sarah, Plain and Tall
Shoeshine Girl
Taste of Blackberries, A

	$51.95
Tax @ 7%	$3.64
S & H @ 10%	$5.20
Total:	**$60.79**

	Quantity	Price	Total	Method of Payment:
4th Grade Book Pack		$51.95		☐ Check
"Unleash the Greatness In Your Child" Workbook Series — Indicate Grade Level		$19.95		☐ Money Order
"I Care" Parental Involvement—Engaging Parents to Improve Student Performance Book ☐ English ☐ Spanish		$14.95		☐ Credit Card

Subtotal
Tax @ 7%
S & H @ $5.00 or 10% (whichever is greater)
Grand Total

Name on Card

Credit Card Number

Expiration Date

Workbook Series

Unleash the Greatness in Your Child Workbook Series $19.95/ea.

Workbook Grade Level	Available
Toddler	July 2006
Pre–Kindergarten	Now
Kindergarten	Now
1st Grade	Now
2nd Grade	Now
3rd Grade	Now
4th Grade	Now
5th Grade	Now
6th Grade	July 2006
7th Grade	September 2006
8th Grade	September 2006
9th Grade	October 2006
10th Grade	October 2006
11th Grade	November 2006
12th Grade	November 2006

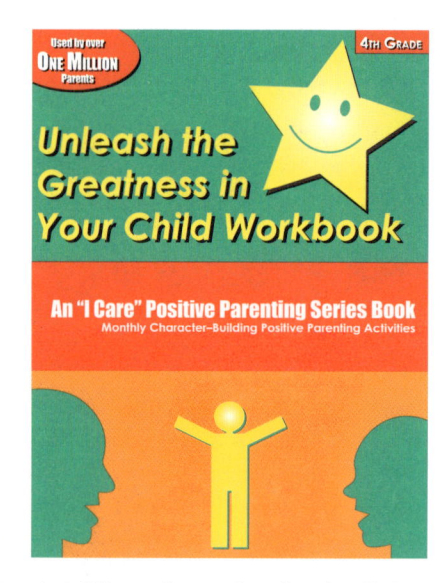

                                               $19.95
Tax @ 7% $1.40
S & H @ $5.00 or 10%
(whichever is greater) $5.00

Total: $26.35

Additional copies for individuals of *Unleash the Greatness in Your Child* Workbooks can be purchased at www.amazon.com, www.borders.com, www.barnesandnoble.com (or www.bn.com), and in Barnes & Noble book stores.

Schools and school systems can order additional copies at www.icarenow.com.

Mail to:

_____
Name

_____
Street Address

_____
City   State   ZIP

_____
Telephone (Optional)

_____
E-mail Address (Optional)

"I Care" Parenting Manual
P.O. Box 492
Americus, GA 31709

50 Ways Parents Can Say "I Care"

1. Post & Discuss Positive Messages
2. Attend Teacher/Parent Conferences
3. Take Family Portraits
4. Post Affirmation Pledges
5. Eat Meals Together
6. Post Daily Schedule
7. Assign Chores
8. Make Scrapbooks Together
9. Cook Meals Together
10. Award Certificates
11. Watch Movies Together
12. Visit Theme Parks
13. Volunteer at School
14. Read Books to Each Other
15. Attend Family Events
16. Give Parties for Special Occasions
17. Schedule Board Game Nights
18. Visit the Zoo
19. Help with a Class Project
20. Monitor TV Programs
21. Attend Parenting Workshops
22. Send Get Well Cards to Friends & Family
23. Lunch with Mom
24. Lunch with Dad
25. Encourage Hobbies
26. Attend Sport Events
27. Attend Local Theatre
28. Provide Enrichment Activities
29. Schedule Ice Cream Socials
30. Visit the Library
31. Go Shopping Together
32. Attend Friends' Events
33. Help with Homework
34. Post a Child Affirmation Pledge
35. Enroll Child in Book Club
36. Go Fishing Together
37. Go Skating Together
38. Encourage Creativity
39. Discuss Child's Day
40. Praise Good Efforts
41. Say *I Love You* Often
42. Write Notes to Recognize Achievement
43. Document Positive Activities
44. Talk About Positive Activities
45. Role Model Desired Behaviors
46. Support Extracurricular Activities
47. Schedule Family Nights
48. Attend Community Events
49. Help with School Projects
50. Set Limits

"I Care" Parental Involvement Book

"I Care" Parental Involvement—Engaging Parents to Improve Student Performance, by Elbert D. Solomon, is full of research–based, field–tested implementation practices and measurement tools and introduces an innovative curricular approach to parental involvement that will delight parents, teachers, and students. More importantly, it will improve student performance, help parents to initiate more positive activities with their children at home, and enable educators to get beyond the difficulties of involving parents. Available in English and Spanish.

	$14.95
Tax @ 7%	$1.05
S & H @ $5.00 or 10% (whichever is greater)	$5.00
Total:	**$21.00**